LIFE BY DESIGN

VOLUME 2

*Restoring the Balance of
Work, Play and Family Life*

Produced by

Kim Ward

Copyright © 2023 by Kim Ward

Publishing all rights reserved worldwide. All rights reserved as sole property of the producer.

The producer guarantees all content is original and does not infringe upon the legal rights of any other person or work.

No part of this book may be reproduced, stored in a retrieval system, or transmitted in any form or by any means, without expressed written permission of the author.

Edited by Lil Barcaski

Published by: GWN Publishing

www.GWNPublishing.com

Cover Design: Kristina Conatser Captured by KC Design

ISBN: 978-1-959608-32-5

This is dedicated to the one I love

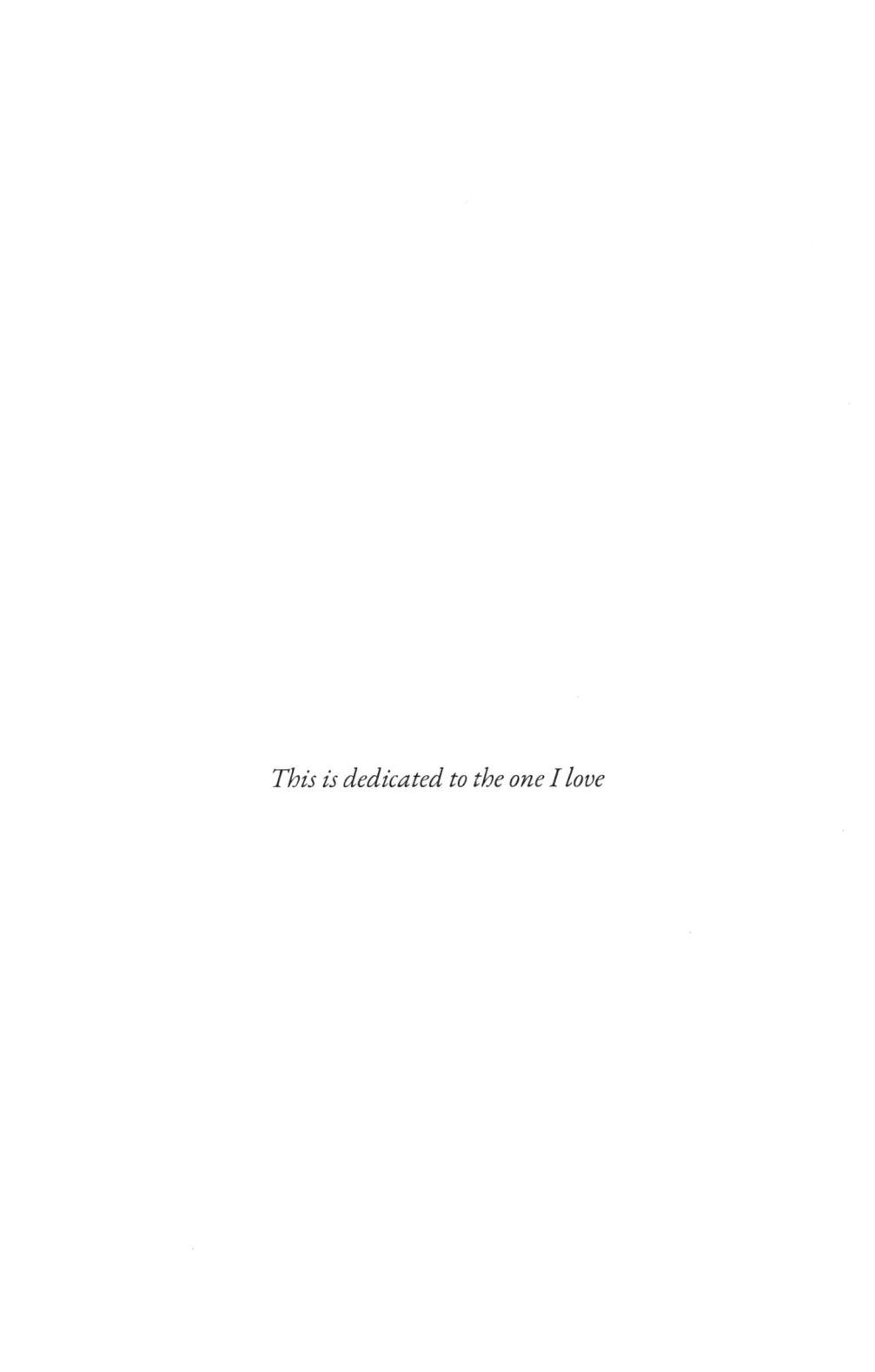

TABLE OF CONTENTS

Leaving A Legacy By Design	*9*
Perfect Work-Life Balance is BS	*19*
Stop Sacrificing You and Live an Intentional Life	*29*
BUSINESS SPOTLIGHT: Allison Grace	*36*
The A, B, Cs of Balance: Accountability, Boundaries, and Compassion	*39*
No One is an Island: Finding Balance in Community	*51*
The Silent Scream of the Soul	*59*
BUSINESS SPOTLIGHT: Lisa T. Daniel	*66*
Chaos to Balance for Peaceful Life	*69*
The Life I Designed	*77*
Aligning With Your Higher Purpose	*87*
Allow Your Passion to Overrule Your Fear	*95*
BUSINESS SPOTLIGHT: Laura Cooke	*104*
Being A Stay-At-Home Mom Is **NOT** What I Signed Up For	*107*
Eat, Play, Action	*113*
Mom, I'm Pregnant... Please, Don't Be Mad	*119*

It's A Miracle That You Are Here. God Must Have Big Plans For You.	*127*
BUSINESS SPOTLIGHT: GWN Publishing, LLC	*132*
BUSINESS SPOTLIGHT: Life By Design Solutions	*134*

Jill Arrington

This chapter is dedicated first to my children and grandchildren who I am leaving this legacy for who undoubtedly are the wind underneath my wings and secondly to my Narcotics Anonymous Family who has shown me so much love and support along my recovery journey.

LEAVING A LEGACY BY DESIGN

Jill Arrington

Hi, my name is Jill Arrington, and I am a grateful, recovering addict with eight years clean, a divorced mom with two adult sons Paul and Edward, six grandchildren (Raydience, Messiah, Jillohn, Azalia, Heaven and Zayden), with a special shout out to my daughter-in-law Sheena. Then there's our dog Hurley and our cat Pepper.

I'm also a successful employee of a major utility company in California who makes a stable six figure income and who has a budding real estate business despite the recessed economy, that's my confession and I'm sticking to it.

I was invited on this journey by Kim, and I was excited about the opportunity to connect with such a Rockstar Entrepreneur and 6 figure earning coach. "Wow! This is so amazing," I thought as I eagerly looked at my budget to make my investment in myself and this once in a lifetime offer. Kim was my social media coach for 6 months and I've been following her ever since. I also wanted to get my feet wet and build some momentum on my dream of writing my own book one day. When I take on any project, I look for something that will stretch me and teach me how to really connect, support and network with people not in my immediate sphere on an authentic level before I say yes. I've been pretty isolated these past two years and I've kept my head down focusing on my one thing… recalibrating my real estate business in a super competitive and sometimes volatile market while working a very demanding job that often required me to work 10-to-12-hour days.

My career was always a major part of my identity and I worked really hard to get to where I am today. However, I climbed the ladder with a lot of baggage due to that fact that I was a recovering addict with several relapses under my belt. I also carried with me this character defect of people pleasing and taking on more that I was able to handle leaving me little time for myself or my family. These behaviors always caused me to play small and come off as the angry black women (even when I wasn't).

The negative mindset that African Americans must work twice as hard and have twice the education in order to excel on the job and be recognized beat me down for half my life. Not that discrimination and racism isn't real, it's just that I allowed it to keep me in overwhelm always feeling like I was different, not enough and that the things in life that I strived for were out of reach no matter how much talent, recovery, education, or money I had. However, there is hope at the end of my story, so please keep reading (smile).

Before I continue with my journey, first I'd like us to look at the definition of **WORK** which is: *the activity involving mental or physical effort done in order to achieve a purpose or result.*

Second, let's look at the definition for the word **LIFE**: *the condition that distinguishes animals and plants from inorganic matter, including the capacity for growth, reproduction, functional activity, and* <u>*continual change preceding death.*</u>

And now, let's look up the word **BALANCE**: *A condition in which different elements are equal or in the correct proportions, an even distribution of weight, enabling someone or something to remain upright and steady.*

Now let's see if we can put it altogether to get a short, clear definition for **WORK LIFE BALANCE**.

> *"The activity involving mental and physical effort done in order to achieve a purpose or result that includes the capacity for growth, reproduction, functional activity, and continual change preceding death that enables someone or something to remain upright and steady."*

As we look into our evolving mental and physical activities in this fast-paced world of technology and inventions today, you see people that struggle to create a sensible work life balance. Here's what I *now* believe, and it made so much sense when I read it.

WORK LIFE BALANCE

> *"Seen as something we ultimately attain, balance is actually something we constantly do. A 'balanced life' is a myth — a misleading concept most accept as a worthy and attainable goal without ever stopping to truly consider it."*
>
> — Gary Keller & Jay Papasan, The ONE Thing

There is no "real" work life balance. Something will always have to take precedence over something else. For example, if I'm working on lead generation for my business. I can't worry about cleaning out my emails or cleaning up my room as it doesn't fit in my tasks for my "One Thing." It has to be a conscious decision to prioritize a task that you scheduled to do. It became when clear when I start focusing on my "One Thing" and got all the side distractions. I got better with cutting out distractions when I carved out time for the other things that mattered in my life so I'm not working from a place of overwhelm and must do's.

Let me give you another example. At first, you may decide to spend a little extra time on your job or career gaining skills, knowledge, going back to school, etc., figuring that if you put in the extra time now, it will pay off later. After a few years of doing that, you may have found yourself working crazy hours in a never-ending pursuit of some business-related goal that never materialized. When you really needed was a mentor to help you get to the next level. While at the same time, family, friends, church, recovery and time for self-care just went out the window with the pursuit of this new career, job, position, etc.

Well, this is what I've done practically my whole life while proudly wearing my Super Woman cape of Type "A", Driver, Overachiever, and Perfectionist behaviors. Always chasing the mighty dollar and the American Dream. I was the "Black Hope" for our family, so I had to become successful and wealthy by any means necessary. So, I just kept adding stuff on my to-do list and putting myself in constant overwhelm and stress. I was always getting ready to get ready. I completed some things, yes, but dropped out of school, stopped going to church and reneged on other positions that I had committed to eventually. I was taking on the world, but at what costs? What was the return on my investment of time, energy, and money? It just wasn't adding up and it became more and more noticeable as I became older.

Yes, I achieved a purpose or result that included the capacity for growth, reproduction, functional activity, and *continual change that almost preceded my death* "literally" that enabled me to remain upright and steady for <u>short periods of time</u> before I would get overwhelmed, give up and relapse on drugs, just to start all over again.

I'm going to take you back to a wonderful scene where I experienced work life balance as an 8-year-old child. My mother and father both worked 8 hr. jobs. My mother worked the night shift as a CNA, and my dad worked the day shift as a janitor for U.C. Berkeley, California, so weekends were our family time. I remember on those weekends no drinking was involved and I had so much peace and stability in my life. I felt loved, secure and safe. We would spend the weekends together either going to the beach or watching National Geographic on the television.

As I grew older, things seemed to become more chaotic and my whole family's dysfunction and mental health challenges progressed and went unchecked. This ended in my brother and sister acting out in school and leaving home by ages 15. This left me feeling alone and sad. I begin taking on some of the adult responsibilities like looking after my niece and calling off for my dad when he was too drunk to go into work.

My life growing up as from a teenager into my adulthood, was especially challenging. I explored things like smoking cigarettes, marijuana and drinking trying to be socially acceptable until crack cocaïne was brought on the scene in the 1980's. I tried crack and for the first time in my life I was spiraling out of control. I've spent half my life running trying to catch up to where I thought I should be emotionally, mentally, and especially financially. My life had become a total mess. I had two sons, one 1983 and 1986. I entered many drug rehabs between 1989 and 1999 and thank God my parents were always there to help me with my children.

Finally, after getting back into recovery in 1999, I managed to get four and a half years clean. Unfortunately, I fell back into my old patterns of work life imbalance. I still hadn't quite surrendered to being an addict and my character defects of perfectionism, being an overachiever, attracting unhealthy relationships and always feeling like I had to be the smartest person in the room to be accepted because I hadn't totally accepted myself got the best of me. My anger and resentment for being an addict was outwardly projected toward God and my family. I despised my life and everyone around me. I didn't understand how this could happen to me and how this could be my journey.

It wasn't until November 1, 2014 that I realized that if I didn't surrender and accept that I was an addict that I was going to be forever trapped in this endless loop of starting over, self-sabotage and possibly death.

Fortunately, I had the mind and clarity to do the "One Thing" I knew could end the negative cycle for good and that was surrender to the fact that I was an addict and accept that for me recovery needed to be at the top of my "One Thing" list for the rest of my life in order to achieve the rest of my things on my "One Thing" list.

Now, I that I've finished sharing the mess. Let me share the message of hope with a short list of things that I do to achieve some resemblance of **WORK LIFE BALANCE.**

1. I focus daily on self-acceptance and the gift of addiction that has allowed me to heal and help so many other fellow addicts on this journey of recovery. **MANTRA:** *It's not too late! God will meet me where I am. My trial can be my testimony based on my positive perception of it.*

2. I accept that I am enough! I don't need not one more degree, career move, business opportunity, or raise! **MANTRA:** *God is the Source of all my needs and everything is always working out for me.*

3. I created a list of my Top 5 things that I am committed to being a part of and focusing on this coming year, but I know that if I start to feel stressed or anxious, I can step down or back and these commitments can easily be served by someone else or taken off the list (with the exception of Recovery). **MANTRA:** *It's great to contribute and serve others, but only when I'm taking excellent care of myself and my family.*

4. I accept that there is no such thing as work life balance, only me choosing to my priorities and giving attention to them. **MANTRA:** *There is nothing more powerful in my life than the power of choice. I am grateful for the privilege.*

Over time, after taking the steps above and embodying my mantras did things begin to change. This year I passed my two-year probation on that 10-12 hr. job and was able to get a bid out to a lateral position with no stress and a minor pay cut that will be replaced with the new year cost of living raise.

In that, I've created more time to spend with family and run my family business so that I can create cash flow assets for retirement through real estate investing while leaving a legacy for my family. I'm going to retire by the time I'm 60 and still have time to travel and enjoy myself! Let's do it!

I'm here for YOU! My purpose IS to help women of color 50 and over create cash flow assets for retirement through real estate investing and leave a legacy for their family. It's a goal that stretches and challenges me. I firmly believe that if I can do it this late in the game so can anyone!

I'd love to share my video with my *free* eBook "*8 Easy Steps to Leaving A Legacy for Your Family - Real Estate Investing for Beginners*" to get you started on your real estate journey.

Here's what you get when you work with me:

- An energized Real Estate Agent with 20+ years of customer service excellence!

- A smooth, hassle-free transaction!

- $2500 Rebate on any purchase or sale over $500K | Using Our Lender

- 0.25% Rebate on any purchase or sale under $500k | Using Our Lender

- Various Loan Options including Down Payment and Closing Cost Assistance for 1st Time Homebuyers | Using Our Lender

- Access to "Free Credit Repair" and affiliate marketing partnership for additional stream of cash flow

- A Free "Leaving A Legacy" Plan (1 hr. consultation) valued at $99.00

Martha Brown

This is dedicated to my husband, Cory, who has shown me over the years that he loves me and our kids, not just in words, but in action. Thank you for loving us the way you do!

PERFECT WORK-LIFE BALANCE IS BS

(I Can Handle It All)

Martha Brown

Do you ever feel like the perfect work-life balance is an unattainable goal? Do you beat yourself up for not being able to do it all, achieving that mythical place of "having it all together"?

As much as society expects us to seek perfectionism in every aspect of our lives, I am here to tell you that **PERFECT WORK-LIFE BALANCE IS BS!**

I have constantly tried to have what one considers perfect balance...you know giving equal time and attention to the different areas in my life...my family, my friends, my work, my health. Talk about **IMPOSSIBLE**! I became drained, overwhelmed, overworked and unhappy. Trying to be everything to everyone, every time was exhausting and when I couldn't do it, I felt terrible about myself. I started drinking more and eventually turned to drugs just to escape the push and pull of not meeting the expectations I had put on myself to be perfectly balanced.

It's when I got sober, that I started to realize that life is more about a blend and if I wanted to be happy and stay sober, I had to kick the high expectations to the curb.

So, I am here to let you know that it's time to relieve some of the guilt of not being able to do it all perfectly and to start letting go of trying to be superwoman.

Instead, let's take a different approach that embraces imperfection and helps us lead a more blended life on our own terms, with ebbs and flows.

IS IT EVEN POSSIBLE TO HAVE A PERFECT BALANCE BETWEEN WORK AND LIFE?

Ah, the age-old quest for the mythical creature known as perfect work-life balance!

It's like searching for a unicorn that's breakdancing on a tightrope. While it might be quite fun to watch, it's important to recognize that achieving an impeccable equilibrium might be just as unreal.

The truth is, our circumstances and priorities are constantly shifting – like the sands of the Sahara, my friends! So instead of chasing after the fantastical idea of a perfect balance, let's embrace the glorious messiness of life and strive for harmony. After all, it's the unexpected wobble in our strides that inspires growth and keeps things delightfully quirky!

There are some days that you simply have to have more focus on one area of your life. Unfortunately, or fortunately depending on how you look at it, the areas of our lives can't be perfectly compartmentalized. So when a kiddo gets sick, you may have to make some shifts for work. Or when a big project is due, you may have to find a sitter for the kids. And it's okay! Really it is. This is how life works.

THE PROS AND CONS OF BEING A WORKAHOLIC

Now I know there are workaholics out there! I am a recovering workaholic and can still slip into this myself some days.

You know who you are. We are the rare individuals who find solace in drowning ourselves in endless tasks and never-ending deadlines. But is being a workaholic really a bed of roses, or a perpetual ride on the roller coaster of burnout?

On one hand, workaholics bask in the glory of accomplishments and climb the ladder of success rather swiftly. Our unyielding passion and dedication often make us experts in our fields, as we continuously strive for growth and improvement.

However, all that glitters is not gold. While our careers flourish, the other aspects of our lives might wilt.

Our relationships, health, and mental well-being often take a backseat as deadlines become unwelcome house guests - overstaying their welcome.

Honestly, my marriage was rocky for a bit when I was constantly working, my husband not knowing what was more important, my job or him. And no matter how often I would tell him, my actions did not show him this, as I would spend hours at work, morning to night, and then come home and still be on the computer or phone about work.

Something had to change or I would lose him. And it was me. I had to change the workaholic mindset that if I didn't do it perfectly, then it wasn't good enough. If I didn't spend every waking hour working, then I wasn't good enough. Woah!

So, the question remains - is being a workaholic worth the trade-offs? Closing one's eyes and taking a leap of faith may just answer that riddle for you. But remember, a healthy blend of different areas in life is the key to savoring a bountiful feast of success, sans the burnout aftertaste.

FINDING TIME FOR SELF CARE DURING BUSY WEEKS

Let's face it, adulting can sometimes feel like we're on a non-stop treadmill going at the speed of light. Our work deadlines, social gatherings, kids' activities, and household chores all blend into one giant whirlwind of busyness, leaving us breathless and exhausted.

However, amidst the pandemonium, self-care should never take a backseat!

A wise person once said, "You can't pour from an empty cup." So, let's fill that cup up, shall we? When life gets chaotic, steal those tiny pockets of time, like the 5 minutes waiting for your morning coffee or the ten minutes between meetings.

Use them to practice mindfulness, express gratitude, or simply take a few deep breaths. Remember, Rome wasn't built in a day, and self-care doesn't always have to be a spa day or a weekend getaway.

These small yet powerful acts of self-love sprinkled across the hustle-bustle of a super productive day will grant you the well-earned, magical touch of relaxation and rejuvenation that you truly deserve. Cheers to finding harmony in the madness!

And I say that, living in complete madness most of the time in my house. Three kids, two dogs, a busy husband, a house to take care of, a business to run and some health issues can all feel like the world is closing in some days. Chaos at its worst, but even in the most chaotic of days, I have found that if I start my morning off with a few key items, such as affirmations, a gratitude list and a bit of planning the day, I feel like I am pouring from a full cup.

Other days, I have to really focus on taking some self-care steps such as taking a few extra minutes in the shower or sitting down with a good book, even turning on some fun music and dancing helps. Self-care doesn't have to be about the big-ticket items, it literally says in the words it is about caring for self. Caring for you!

WHAT DOES YOUR IDEAL WEEK LOOK LIKE

Imagine waking up to the melodies of birds chirping, the sun gently kissing your skin, and the aroma of freshly brewed coffee, welcoming you to a week that is nothing short of pure bliss.

Your ideal week is an impeccable blend of productivity, indulgence, and adventure. Days spent conquering goals with the focus and finesse of a ninja, followed by evenings unwinding with a captivating book, or painting the town red with your vibrant squad.

Your weekends are an epic medley of adrenaline-pumping escapades and serene moments spent basking in nature's beauty or curled up in a blanket fort while losing yourself in your favorite TV show. Each day is filled with laughter, love, and learning—and living your ideal week fuels your soul and leaves you inspired to chase the life of your dreams.

Sounds incredible doesn't it! If only life could be that perfect, but in recognizing that life isn't perfectly balanced, we can bring in these moments to our days to start having more and more of what we would love an ideal day to be.

There are always going to be bumps in the roads that can tip the scales and that's why when you try to hold onto the balance so hard you can end up hurting yourself, mentally, physically and spiritually.

HOW TO PRIORITIZE TASKS TO MAXIMIZE PRODUCTIVITY

In the whirlwind of life, it can feel like there is a never-ending pile of tasks to accomplish, causing chaos to reign like confetti at a parade. But fear not, productivity warriors!

With a few mindful adjustments, you can rise above the bedlam, and conquer the art of prioritizing tasks. Sharpen your creative wit and wrangle that to-do list into submission by identifying your most pivotal tasks and slaying those dragons first, unlocking legendary levels of productivity, like a video game. If you are anything like me, just crossing off those tasks, help me to feel more productive.

I even start my week with a brain dump of all the things I need to get done for the week. I set a timer for 10 minutes and with a pen and paper just write out anything that comes to mind. When the timer goes off, I go back over the list and circle the top three items I need to get done for the week and then fill in the rest. Since starting this, it has helped me so much to not beat myself up.

I would also like to invite you to embrace the power of delegation, because even the mightiest of heroes need a trusty sidekick.

Finally, remember to savor the sweet taste of victory by rewarding yourself upon completion of each milestone. By mastering the art of prioritization, you shall transform into an unstoppable force of efficiency, a champion of productivity, and a titan of time management.

MAKING TIME FOR FUN IN THE MIDST OF THE HUSTLE AND BUSTLE

In the whirlwind of daily life, we often find ourselves swept up in endless to-do lists, appointments, and deadlines. This can be all-consuming, as we dance between obligations and responsibilities.

But lo and behold! There's an antidote to the hustle and bustle – the secret sauce that keeps us humans sane, happy, and ready for more: FUN!

That's right, my fellow life-jugglers, making time for enjoyment is not only essential but absolutely doable, even amid the craziness of our busy schedules. It's about being creative, seizing those spontaneous moments to laugh, dance or escape into a gripping novel. Remember, we're not mere work drones, destined for a life of monotony!

We have an inner spark that thrives on excitement and amusement, so let's feed that flame, embrace the unruly, and infuse our daily grind with gleeful mayhem. And with that, I challenge you to unleash your inner fun-seeker and surely, you'll witness your life transform, one delightful moment at a time.

We can all agree that having a perfect balance between work and life is almost impossible, so why not use the pros of being a workaholic to our advantage? It's okay to hustle and bustle—as long as we don't forget to have some fun too!

Making time for self-care during busy weeks, knowing what our ideal week looks like, and prioritizing tasks to maximize productivity while at work can help us find a better blend between work and life, however, having an understanding that if we live our life like a perfectly lined up row of dominoes, then just one small breeze can disrupt it all and everything, including you will crash down.

When you leave room for the ebbs and flows in life, giving yourself grace when taking moments for self-care or an extra moment of fun, you can breathe a little easier and even be happier in life.

Or when things don't go as planned, or you yell way too loudly at your kids, know that we all make mistakes and we all need help sometimes.

HERE ARE A FEW OF MY BEST TIPS TO CREATING AN INCREDIBLE BLENDED LIFE FOR YOU:

1. **UNPLUG FROM TECHNOLOGY ON A REGULAR BASIS.** This may be some time you take daily or weekly, whatever works best for you.

2. **IN THE MORNING, SET UP A ROUTINE THAT WORKS FOR YOU,** but includes moments for you to get into a space to take on the day and start it in a positive light. Some ideas include using affirmations, a gratitude list, meditation or journaling.

3. **SETTING BOUNDARIES.** It's okay to say NO! Take a look at your why before you agree to something.

So go ahead and conquer your goals, but don't forget the important things in life like family, good friends, and looking after oneself!

I also want to invite you to learn more at http://successwithmarthabrown.com where you can create a life that excites you to get out of bed in the morning.

WEBSITE: https://marthabrowncoaching.com/
EMAIL: martha@marthabrowncoaching.com

Cheryl Cobbin

To my family without whom I would not have had the life experiences to share in this book.

STOP SACRIFICING YOU AND LIVE AN INTENTIONAL LIFE

Cheryl Cobbin

I help entrepreneurs and small businesses protect their business assets as well as their personal identity. I've got you covered from forming your business to scaling your business. I especially enjoy helping women create a life by their own design!

I'm sure you've heard the phrase "You can't do it all." But have you ever really thought about what that means?

Ten years ago, if you would've told me that I would be where I am now, I would have told you that it wasn't going to happen. After getting married and having my daughters, I was so excited to be a Mom. I loved staying home and raising them while they were young, but eventually they got older and were doing their own thing. Then it hit me: I needed something different than being a stay-at-home Mom. I began questioning my identity.

So, here's what happened next: my volunteering in the classroom led to teaching. I really enjoyed making a difference with my students while working as a teacher for quite a number of years. Then I realized that I was once again in a space of caregiving—not caretaking! —and not caring for myself as much as I needed to be. And I still had that feeling I could be doing something different. Something more?

I started to feel like I was losing myself, again.

It was a gradual thing, but it started to happen. I'd wake up and think "What am I really doing?" or "What have I become?" I started to feel like my identity was being stripped away from me, and the more I struggled to hold onto it, the more it slipped through my fingers.

I felt like I had sacrificed everything that made me who I am—and what's worse, nobody even noticed! I needed to re-discover me. It took a lot of thinking, and some serious soul searching before I realized what was happening: there was a need to have more balance in my life.

I couldn't just sit back and let things happen anymore—I had to take action!

So, I decided to take control of my life by starting my own business. This was for me, for the first time in a very long time!

I found an amazing community of people that were like me; entrepreneurs facing an array of adult challenges. My social life was now meeting new people and attending networking events. I felt the change in me happening, finally figuring out who I was again.

When people ask me what running my own business is all about, all I can say is that it's about being yourself again—it's about having a supportive community around you; it's about knowing where your place in life is supposed to be... but most importantly? It's about finding a way for you as an individual person to connect with other like-minded people.

It is a lot of hard work but the freedom and the ability to live life on my own terms is worth all the work that I do in my business. **It does not define who I am. I define who I am**. And running a business is just part of that. I am creating a life by my own design.

While figuring all of this out, the pandemic hit.

During first part of 2020, I was really struggling because things had changed so much. I had wrapped myself into networking as my main marketing strategy and being heavily involved in my chamber, while serving as an ambassador. With all the social and in-person events coming to an abrupt halt, I had to re-invent and shift to virtual networking. That was quite the challenge!

It was also a time of reflection about my life, my purpose.

Everything I had done up this point was serving others - putting my husband and girls first; they were my big rocks. Then my teaching, along with the chamber and networking were the pebbles. My self-care, my self-development, my evolving career, really all of it, was like the sand that filled in around it.

I've always known I wanted to be an entrepreneur. But it took me a long time to realize that I was one.

While I was busy raising my kids, I never understood how to find the time or space to think about starting a business. And even when I did get started, I found myself feeling guilty that the time I spent working on my business should have been doing something else for others, my family.... really anyone else.

What I realized is that it's OK not to do everything.

And now that the girls are older, I can see that there is no right way to be a Mother or an Entrepreneur. The only thing that matters is doing what you love and being true to yourself and your values. You don't have to choose between your kids and your career; you can have both!

Staying true to yourself, there's no limit on how far you can go in this world. Knowing that you can do anything at any age; knowing that you shouldn't put limits on yourself; knowing that you are the one who can self-sabotage yourself; and knowing that you are the one who can make changes at any time.

When I have a better balance and understanding of all that is going around me, it makes it a lot easier to incorporate things into my life that I love and enjoy.

I've taught my daughters that the world isn't just about them—it also is about what can we do for the world. We are a serving family, and in the end that is how I've become a servant leader.

The biggest thing that I have learned in all of this is that I cannot serve others without first taking care of me. Taking that time without guilt, I'm able to feel that value… I'm able to find my own path… I'm able to open doors to other possibilities.

In society we have these different mommy and socializing groups… from Mothers of Preschoolers (MOPS) to Girl Scouts to National Charity League (NCL). They are all incredible, but every group that I was part of was for my girls, not necessarily for me—and that's another place a shift needed to happen. I needed to add something for me, without feeling the guilt.

I also think I struggled so much with this because growing up I moved a lot.

From the age of six to thirteen, I never stayed in any place for a very long period of time. This meant that during those pivotal years, I didn't have any childhood friends to rely on—I had to rely on my siblings instead, as developing relationships that would not possibly last was painful.

Because of all of that moving, I never laid down roots. When I became a parent, it was important for my children to develop long term relationships with other families in the neighborhood. I wanted them to experience what I hadn't as a child.

As an entrepreneur, I started to cultivate adult relationships. The way I did this was through networking, meeting new people, making new connections, and actively being involved with my chamber.

All these experiences are what shaped many of my values: serving, reliability, dependability, and integrity/character.

Life is about trying to balance things out but it's not always about perfect balance—it's about weaving in the ebb and flow within different areas of your life. You must stop and take time to care for yourself, otherwise you will burn out and won't be able to serve those around you who mean the most... your family, friends, and clients!

Passion is the new energy that fuels me. I have learned to set my goals by breaking them down into manageable steps, where I am building them one brick at a time.

I have implemented self-care into my life. I protect the time I wake up until I am ready to begin my business day with exercise, journaling, and listening to great audios to help get my mindset straight. I pamper myself regularly with massages, facials, and pedicures.

What I want for you is to know:

1. Self-care and knowing who you are during all those roles you play in life are important to your mental health.
2. When discovering or even rediscovering who you are, it's okay to set boundaries without feeling guilt.
3. Spend time cultivating the relationships that are important to you.
4. You can start anything at any age.
5. YOU deserve to feel your best, work as the best you AND give yourself time and space to be healthy.

Practicing these things will allow you to show up authentically and fully serve those you care for and those who need you.

It's the balance of knowing who you are so you can prioritize what needs to happen with grace, and place focus on cultivating the relationships and community around you.

To learn more about the author, check out my info at https://www.inphone.co/cc

EMAIL: cheryl@cherylcobbin.com/
LINKLIST: linktr.ee/cherylcobbin
FACEBOOK: https://www.facebook.com/profile.php?id=100000069214425/
LINKEDIN: https://www.linkedin.com/in/cherylcobbin/
PINTEREST: https://www.pinterest.com/CherylCobbinBusiness/

BUSINESS SPOTLIGHT

Allison Grace

I help teens and young adults reduce their anxiety
and improve their focus and mental clarity.

I'm Allison Grace and I am a mental wellness coach that helps my clients feel better in their own skin by using holistic protocols and one-one coaching to help them thrive.

I work with people with ADHD, depression, anxiety, autoimmune diseases, intrusive thoughts, someone with a special need sibling or family, tics, and athletes, and even dancers.

I have suffered from those, so they are dear to my heart, but I am willing to help anyone get to their best self by getting their physical, mental, and even financial wellness to 100 percent, so you can feel amazing, and you can be the happy and healthy person you strive to be.

Please connect with me by clicking on my QR code where you can find all my contact information.

Laura Cooke

To all you ladies who are giving it your all every day: may you find the peace, rest, and balance you deserve.

THE A, B, CS OF BALANCE: ACCOUNTABILITY, BOUNDARIES, AND COMPASSION

Managing body, mind and soul to create balance while pursuing your passions

Laura Cooke

Exhaustion. We wear it like a badge of honor. We're raised to work hard, serve everyone, keep organized, nurture the family, take care of the pets. But we do so at our own expense. Burn out is taking a toll and it has really destructive effects on our psyche, productivity, and health.

As women, we often ignore our own needs to ensure everyone around us is cared for. We'll stretch ourselves, push ourselves, and neglect ourselves to serve our work, our families, our friends, our parents, our community, and our causes. When we finally do get a moment to ourselves, we end up forcing relaxation through television, wine, scrolling through social media, online shopping, or other unproductive behaviors and then we feel guilty about how we've spent our down time. We worry about everyone else's health but we don't allow ourselves the space for exercise, care, or restoration.

If you can relate, I am here to tell you, you are not alone. We are conditioned to give until it hurts, and then reward ourselves only once everything is done. Our concept of reward is based on indulging in those unproductive behaviors that numb rather than restore, and instead we leave the day even MORE depleted after our perceived "break".

This pattern can work for a time, but eventually it catches up with us. Our bodies shut down, we develop anxiety or depression, or even worse, we die younger than we should.

As someone who struggles with balance, I get YOU. It has taken YEARS of practice to manage the expectations I place on myself and others. The most profound lesson I have learned is that you have to have a full cup in order to properly serve and give to others. If we do not first ensure we are taken care of, we're managing through life frenzied, resentful, and only partially present. We are going through the motions rather than really connecting and making an impact in our relationships, work, or communities.

As a consultant, I have studied many models for effective leadership, and I came to realize that leading self is as important as leading a team, family, organization, or community. What I've discovered is:

YOU NEED TO PUT YOUR OWN OXYGEN MASK ON FIRST

To encourage balance for our loved ones, we need to model that for them to see. How will our daughters learn to take time for themselves if we don't show them what that looks like? How will they be healthy, happy, and fulfilled if we teach them that our needs as women come last? I've broken it into the ABCs of balance: Accountability, Boundaries, and Compassion to fully start realizing that in order to help and serve, we must first help ourselves. Let's unpack what that looks like.

ACCOUNTABILITY

This is a tricky one. We are often hard enough on ourselves that we consider ourselves accountable. The question I'll ask you though is, "Do you hold yourself accountable towards your own well-being"? If it is truly our job to care for others, how can we do that if we're not well enough to care for ourselves? Who takes care of our family if we become ill or worse? How can we create a new model of Accountability that serves US so we may serve others? Let's look at the three elements of wellbeing and how we might adapt a new model for accountability.

Body:

Our ability to contribute to our families, our workplaces and our communities relies on our wellness. How can we take time out for wellness to ensure we have the energy to take care of everything we have on our plates? Here are some ideas.

Book time for movement: As women, exercise is the key to wellbeing – especially as we age. Rather than thinking about the time we don't have. Ask yourself "How much time do I have and what can I do in that amount of time?" Where can you fit some movement into your life? What kind of movement do you enjoy?

At home:

- Can you get up a half an hour earlier and go for a walk?
- Can you meet a friend and go for an exercise class even just one day a week?
- Is there a sport you might like to take up as a family (pickleball, skiing, soccer, Friday night dance parties)?
- What movement doesn't feel like "work" or a "chore" to you?

At work:

- If in the office/on premise, can you have a walking meeting rather than a sit-down meeting?
- Are there stairs you can take? How many will you do? I had a rule that if my meeting was within three flights up or five flights down, I would take the stairs.
- Can you take half of your lunchtime for exercise and half of the time to eat?
- Do you have a standing desk?
- Can you do some chair yoga?

In terms of nutrition, what are you putting into your body? How can you make one small change to improve what you are consuming? You don't have to change it all, one small step over time can have amazing impact. One less coffee, twice the vegetables, reducing your carbohydrate consumption, what can you do that doesn't feel like a punishment to start?

What part do the others in your workplace, family, friendships play in support of your wellness? Where can you build and hold accountability in others so that you are a priority on your list? Here are some questions to get you thinking:

- What tasks are on your list that you could delegate to others?
- What if you didn't swoop in and fix something the next time someone else falls short?
- What can you request of others to allow love and caring to be returned?
- What can you teach someone so that it can come off your plate?

Mind:

What needs to shift for you to make movement a positive thing? Can you pair your morning treadmill with your favorite guilty pleasure show, podcast or playlist? How might you reward yourself differently? Can exercise time replace the unproductive behaviors we do instead? What is your relationship to food? What is one thing you can improve or change without it feeling like a punishment?

Spirit:

What motivates you? Do you need an accountability partner to help stay on track? I recommend finding someone who is equally motivated, committed, and is far enough away from friendship that you will only spend 5-10 minutes checking in at the start of each day. Do you need tough love, encouragement or a mixture of both? Be sure to ask for what you need.

BOUNDARIES

Boundaries are the hand rails for staying on track. Boundaries are a way of protecting what's important and communicating our limits. Boundaries are the strings that hold the scale of balance. When they break, so does our resolve, our protection of self, and our well-being. So, why are they so hard to set and even harder hold? They feel selfish and they are difficult to communicate because we have to own our stance (rather than smile and feel resentment on the inside). Setting and holding boundaries is one of the bravest and most difficult way to protect your balance. They are also the most effective.

So, what do boundaries look like when we hold them up against our three elements?

Body:

What limits does your body have? Where do you need to push and where do you need to give? What is your hard stop for putting work, kids, chores, and giving down? How much sleep do you need? How will you protect that? What sign posts does your body have to tell you, "enough" or "too much"?

When we listen to our bodies, we can learn to regulate in a way that honors healthy striving or pushing AND rest and recovery.

To help you find your body's wisdom, ask yourself this and notice how it shows up in your body:

- When I am stressed, my body feels....

- When I am healthy, my body feels....

- To relieve stress, my body needs…
- To protect or improve my health, my body needs.…

Mind:

Sometimes that inner voice can be the most detrimental to our well-being. We have to learn to set boundaries in our mind to encourage the thoughts that drive the behaviors we want to build. When we're busy, our minds are busy, and it's sometimes difficult to quiet that voice. We run lists, scenarios, worries, and plans constantly so that even when our bodies are quiet, our minds are still racing.

How do we quiet these thoughts that rob us of peace? I have a few suggestions that might work for you:

- Keep your voice memo app or notebook near you at all times. Next time something pops up, note it and let it go. It's when we try to hold things in memory that we keep our minds busy. Once we have "dealt" with it, our minds relax.

- If you are sleeping, you can do the same. If an urgent task you forgot about pops into your head, write it down or note it in your app so your mind can let go.

- If you are having trouble sleeping because your mind is racing, take each thought, imagine it in your hands, and then imagine placing that thought on a leaf that is floating down a stream. Let the stream carry that thought away. Repeat this for each new thought that occurs.

Spirit:

What boundaries do you need to put in place to make time for you to connect with yourself? Can you take 10 minutes a day to get quiet and mindful? What does connecting to spirit look like for you? Do you like to journal, tune into your inner wisdom, pray or something else? What does it feel like for you to connect in this way? How does it help you be a better leader, mother, wife, friend? Can you put time for this kind of connection in your schedule?

COMPASSION

Compassion is the key to the human experience. When we talk about balance, compassion is the sacred space between healthy striving and being too hard on ourselves. Compassion in itself is a balance as it is not always clear when we need to extend it to others or ourselves. Compassion is also the greatest gift in that the grace we extend to others, is also a gift to us.

Body:

It's often difficult to look upon ourselves with compassion. We are programmed to expect to see perfection and yet the beauty of the human race is that we are imperfect by nature. What comes to mind when you look at yourself in the mirror? Do you have those terrible voices of self-criticism or do you hear kind and gentle thoughts? Compassion in and for your body can look like this:

- Extending love and wellness to any part of your body that feels unwell

- Reprogramming the critical voice in our heads by finding one thing you are happy with
- Learning when to push and when to rest and extending compassion to ourselves regardless of the choice (even if it was the wrong one)

Mind:

Compassion in our minds can be equally difficult. We, as humans, are built to place judgment on ourselves and others based on our past experiences, values, and patterns. When we catch ourselves judging others, it can be helpful to ask, "what is a more generous and loving interpretation of what I just experienced or thought?" When I find myself thinking those harsh words of self-criticism, I try to catch myself and ask, "What's a kinder, gentler way of saying that to yourself?" or "What would you say to a friend in the same circumstance?"

Spirit:

Building a compassionate spirit is a practice. It starts with understanding that when we judge, the burden is on OUR shoulders. We carry the weight and consequence of those tough thoughts. Learning to let go is freedom, weightlessness, and joy. Compassion is not an act for others – is it an act for self.

If anything resonated for you here, I invite you to find ONE thing you can do to bring more balance to your life. One thing done consistently over time creates a habit. One habit after another creates transformation. You deserve it!

Do you need help making a plan for balance in your life? Scan my QR code at the beginning of this chapter to schedule a complimentary Balance Blueprint session with me today to make a customized plan to bring balance to your day.

Mitch Creedy

I dedicate this chapter to my loving partner for her unwavering support. Thank you for always being there for me and for being the constant cheerleader by my side.

NO ONE IS AN ISLAND: FINDING BALANCE IN COMMUNITY

Mitch Creedy

Finding balance in life can be extremely challenging nowadays! There are many demands on our time and everyone wants a little piece of us. Can you relate? Not only do we have our immediate lives to live, but we also have online groups and commitments which seem to be getting more numerous as time goes by. For people living with disabilities, there are the usual pressures like family and life in general and then, there's the issue of adapting activities so that they work for us. How do we find the time and energy to do the things we need to do while living the lives we want? In this chapter, I'd like to speak specifically to the reality of living a life in balance life while living the life you want with a disability.

Hi, my name is Mitch and I'm blind. I identify as non-binary and use they/them pronouns. Few, talk about intersectionality!

I grew up in South Africa and moved to Canada at the age of 16. Growing up in South Africa, I attended a school for the blind but after moving to Canada, I attended a local high school in my community and had to figure out how to balance the after-school activities I wanted to be a part of while managing school and homework. Sounds like any other teenager, doesn't it? In those days, we didn't have all the fancy technology we have now. Completing homework sometimes took me two to three times longer than my sighted peers. I don't tell you this so you will feel sorry for me! I'm not looking to be anyone's inspiration. I only mention this to illustrate how I came to learn about balancing life at such a young age.

When most people think about balance, they tend to think about balancing school, work, family, self-care, and spending time with friends. All of these factors are important, and living a life in balance certainly means balancing all of these things. When thinking about balance from the lens of disability, I'd like to offer an additional perspective.

There is this idea out there that the most successful people with disabilities are the people who do it all! They are the ones who are fiercely independent and who don't take assistance even if the task takes them three times longer to complete. This is the standard to which we are all encouraged to aspire. How do I know? I was one of those people! I was going to do it all by myself, and for a while, that worked out for me… until it didn't.

I was having coffee with a friend one day when she remarked that I might want to consider allowing other people to help me. I tend to have a difficult relationship with the word "help," and prefer to use support or accompany. Help has such negative connotations for those of us who have been subjected to the charity model of supporting the blind that still exists in Canada. I immediately got annoyed with my friend and began explaining all the reasons why I didn't need help. I was capable of doing things on my own and sighted people jump in way too quickly to help. I went on my way determined to do everything by myself even more than before.

A few months later, I was attending a meeting when a blind friend of mine casually mentioned that they didn't mind having support as long as it was their choice and on their terms. What did that mean anyway? Little did I know that I'd soon find out.

Enter pandemic times! All of a sudden, no one wanted to assist me in the stores. Customer service support for shopping was hard to come by. My partner or someone else in my bubble had to take me everywhere, and I certainly wasn't comfortable taking the bus at that point. Sighted guide was off the table because walking that close to someone outside of my bubble wasn't something I felt safe doing. I had compromised lungs when I was younger and so I consciously made these decisions to keep myself safe. The days of asking for directions were over because others had their own reasons for staying away from people. Some of the online platforms for grocery shopping were not accessible and there was nothing anyone wanted to do about it. I couldn't even take a COVID test on my own without someone to read the instructions and the test results.

In the beginning, I thought the pandemic would only last a couple of weeks or months at most, so I just enjoyed the ride. I joined an online yoga group for the blind and happily worked from home. By the fall of 2020, I'd had enough! I felt trapped and didn't know how to live with this new reality. I tried going into a local café and soon realized that everyone was making a wide birth around me. I was having trouble determining which counter to go to due to the glass which was hard to hear through. I wasn't having a particularly good strategizing day and perhaps it was simply that I'd had enough of it all.

It was around this time that I recalled some wise words from the late Archbishop Desmond Tutu who taught and wrote about the concept of Ubuntu. The idea is that none of us are an island unto ourselves. We can't do anything without one another. If I win first prize at a music competition, I'm not winning that prize on my own. I have a teacher who has taught me and mentored me, I have a partner who has supported my practice times, and I have friends who have come to support me at the competition. We are all inter-dependent. I've always like this concept and In my mind, the more community I create, the better off I am and the more I can enrich other people's lives. Coming back to this realization of Ubuntu again made me realize that I need to live this out in my own life.

If I take this concept to heart as a blind person, I'm no different than anyone else. It takes an entire community to support us in whatever we're doing whether we can see or not. The cultural context in which I find myself has taken the concept of independence so far that it has become unhealthy. No one can live as if they are an island! While I might feel that I'm a burden to the person who is coming to the store with me to read ingredients, they might see it as a wonderful opportunity to connect with me. Perhaps they are lonely and appreciate having someone to talk to. Sure, I could go ahead and read the ingredients on that jar with an app on my phone, but I can also choose not to do so. If I learn the blindness skills I need, I get to decide what feels best in terms of completing tasks. It's all about how much energy I want to put in and how much I want to share the task so that I have more energy for other things.

I was out having coffee with the same friend two years later. I told her about how much our conversation before the pandemic had changed my life. I hadn't realized how much I'd bought into this concept of doing everything myself. I certainly grew up doing things with other people and I find myself missing being in community with others. Now, it's something I yearn for.

Many people with disabilities are now creating their own income opportunities which adds another layer to the mix of life activities to balance. Some days are more hectic than others, some days we have more energy than others, and other days are filled with technological accessibility nightmares. The good news is that you don't have to do it all alone! Here are a few strategies we might all want to keep in mind.

Give yourself the grace not to do everything every day. Instead of a daily method of operation for your business, why not develop a weekly method of operation? That way, you have certain tasks you want to do every week. If you are not feeling up to it one day, that's okay. You can move some of the tasks from one day to the next. If you choose to build community around you, you can even trade skills and talents to get things done. For example, I'm no good at creating graphics on the computer and I bake delicious cookies and cakes. My friend loves designing graphics but dislikes baking. The great thing is that they love eating my baking so trading cookies for a graphic is a good deal for both of us.

If it no longer serves you, don't do it anymore. I can't tell you the number of times I've signed up for a course or a business opportunity only to find out that it wasn't accessible or that people were not interested in making it accessible. I hung on to these business opportunities because I thought I could make it work, but in the end, I just had to let it all go. There's something so freeing about letting go of that which no longer serves us. I call it getting into "get rid of it, mode." The beautiful thing is, that when we let go of things that no longer serve us, we make room for new opportunities. There's something quite spiritual that happens when we take out the old and bring in the new.

Take time for spirituality. Sometimes, when people think about spirituality, they think only about organized religion. While organized religion can certainly be part of spirituality, the concept can encompass so much more. Spending time in nature, meditating, doing creative arts like music or painting, and doing mindful activities can all be a part of our spirituality. It's all about calming the mind so that we can feel those nudges from Source, Spirit, the Universe, God, yourself, or whatever you want to call it. One of my favourite spiritual practices is to sit and quiet my mind with a grounding exercise and then to simply write down everything that comes to mind. I think of a question and set an intention for the activity and let whatever comes flow out onto the paper or the computer. It's truly amazing what kinds of answers I have come up with by doing this simple exercise.

There's no "right" way to live life. We all have to do what works for us. I hope that this chapter has given you a few ideas and strategies for creating a life in balance when one of the pieces you're balancing is a disability.

If you would like to stay in touch or if you would enjoy learning more strategies, you are welcome to download my small eBook entitled, *Yes You Can*. It can be found by clicking on the link provided. You are also more than welcome to join my Facebook group for entrepreneurs with disabilities which you can also find out about by clicking on this link.

It's been wonderful sharing with you and I hope you get in touch. I'd love to hear from you.

Would you like to stay connected? Are you someone with a disability who has started or who is thinking of starting your own business? Download my free eBook *Yes You Can*. This one-of-a-kind eBook will help you to learn simple steps you can take daily to grow your business and encourage you to love yourself through those times when you just can't quite make those steps happen. I'm looking forward to connecting!

https://offer.successwithmitch.com/book

Marcia Domecq

This chapter is dedicated to the love and support of my Facebook community and to my faith in Jesus Christ. You kept me afloat when my body and mind was literally falling apart. I am forever grateful.

THE SILENT SCREAM OF THE SOUL

Marcia Domecq

The ice on the road was thick. I knew it was going to be a long four-hour drive home, but I don't remember any of it. I had just received news that my brain tumor, while not cancerous, was life-threatening if it continued growing at its current pace. My body was locked in freeze and my breath was shallow. My mind was blank. I could feel the disconnect between my body and soul, and the present, but I had no words to express what was to come. I was a woman, which meant I had obligations. There is no time to be sick. For women, there are no contingency plans that involve stopping. We are not conditioned for this. We are told to put on our own oxygen mask in the event of an airplane accident, but put us in this kind of scenario and see what we do. In the high of stress, it is instinctual, it is primal, it is imperative to save our children first. It is our automatic go to. So, without thinking, I went on autopilot as, "shit needed to get done." I couldn't remain in freeze mode, so I transitioned into flight ***and*** fight.

But what does flight and fight mean as a woman? It means that we pull ourselves up by our bootstraps. We put a smile on our face and appear to have it all together. We push away the fears and concerns, and concentrate instead on others, and we continue to work until our body slowly falls apart. So, I did what I knew best, I researched the odds of surgery and radiation. I woke at 3 AM and Googled the neurological symptoms that my doctors could not explain. I continued working full time, day in and day out. Never complaining, never feeling sorry for myself, never asking for time off. Because that's what strong women do, right? Meanwhile, there was a silent scream deep within my soul and it literally was tearing my body apart.

I could feel what was happening, but felt powerless to make it stop. I heard the loud tinnitus that rang in my left ear; a result of my Gamma Knife surgery. It continues, even today, 24/7, as if someone is screaming at you at high pitch continually. The conversations with the doctors went something like this.

"There is no treatment or cure and you must ignore it." I noticed that music would never be the same due to the hearing loss from the radiation. And should you complain when you lose 30% hearing when you re-gained 10% with three weeks of high dose prednisone? "You are lucky, don't you know? It could have been worse."

So, you enjoy that small victory while statistics predict you will be entirely deaf in that ear in ten years as a result of the surgery. But the tumor, while still there and frozen, is no longer life-threatening. That is, as long as it doesn't decide to start growing again.

"And those hot burning feet? We could give you some patches for those and some Gabapentin for the continual muscle twitches, pins, and needles. It won't cure anything, but just might cover up some of those symptoms. And the 24/7 internal tremors? Sorry, our instruments don't measure those, so we really don't have any thoughts on those. And even though I don't have answers for those things, I really won't need to see you back for any follow up. Those red patches of psoriasis? Oh, yeah, those look pretty nasty. We aren't really interested in finding out how those or any of these other symptoms came about, and we can't really explain how someone who was completely healthy one day became terribly sick the next. But we really are not paid to search for the root cause. Google? Oh no, don't do that. It can really take you down the rabbit hole. Support groups? I'm not really sure. Maybe you can look something up on Facebook. But don't expect to find the true answers there as it isn't backed by clinical research. Oh, your rare neuromuscular disorder, Myotonia Congenita. Yes, I know you signed up to provide information for clinical research on that, but we really won't be having anyone follow up with you even though you volunteered and filled out a patient permission form. In fact, we won't be having anyone follow up with you at all, yet we will give you appointments at Mayo in five different departments. What, a social worker or psychologist to help you navigate all of this? Well, we really don't have a social worker that does that. Maybe if you had cancer or something. I could put a referral in for you for a psychologist, but most likely you will get an intern. Oh, and that fast-progressing Rheumatoid Arthritis? Yeah, that really sucks. I am pretty concerned about you because your numbers are doubling in your blood tests, so I want you on medications right away. You know there is only a small period of time that the meds can stop the progression of this and if you miss that window of opportunity, then the medication won't be able to help. What? You are wondering if you can only take the medication for a short period of time, just long enough to shut it off? Oh, no. This is medication that you will be on the rest of your life. Side effects, you ask? Well, it is really rare, but it is possible in about 10 years the medication could affect your eyes."

These words went round and round in my head. The surgery had taken my hearing, and now there was a chance the medication could take my eyesight? I looked around for support and saw nothing and no one. I only saw the written appointments on a calendar and doctors who really didn't care if I showed or not. I also observed no multidisciplinary team. No coordination amongst the different departments to discuss my case and certainly, no cheerleader telling me "I got you." I only saw portal reminders of the upcoming appointments and my calendar helping me try to navigate work/home and doctor's visits. There was no stopping, there was no self-care, there were no answers. So, I did what I had to do. I did what any strong woman would do. I decided to take matters into my own hands. The next year of my life was a whirlwind. A non-stop f'ing explosion of activity. I started by refusing any/all medication. I don't suggest this for everyone, but it was the right decision for me. With all my systems offline, I thought, "How am I ever going to get a correct diagnosis if they are chasing side effects from all these meds?" I started researching and digging deep into nutrition, exercise, meditation, and any alternative form of treatment possible. My lunch hours, breaks, evenings, and nights were filled with consuming information. I worked during the day, and went to two, sometimes three, doctor's appointments every night after work. I hit it hard with all kinds of alternative treatments, doing Occupational and Physical Therapy, Chiropractic, and Acupuncture along with my regularly scheduled doctor's appointments. I invested in machines to stimulate my feet that had gone numb and in graston tools to bring back the sensory sensitivities/overload in my hands and arms. I strapped metal braces on my arms at night so that my hands were not numb when I woke in the morning. I used my CPAP, so that my brain and body could get oxygen due to my sleep apnea. I took vitamins and supplements to ward off sudden fatigue and keep my body going. I learned chiropractic exercises to strengthen my body. I found non-medicated neurotech wear and used stem-cell rejuvenation to repair damage. My world was consumed with education and activities of rebuilding my body, mind and spirit.

But to my dismay, even with all these things, I found that I still could not breathe. Upon digging deeper, I discovered layers upon layers of stressors. Financial, relational, work, kids, spouse, Covid, isolation, shut downs, and all the things. This all happened at the height of Covid, while my daughter's college was being shut down not only due to the pandemic, but also due to the fires, rioting, and tear gas by her campus which was three hours away in Minneapolis. My doctor's appointments included hotel stays where they announced there was no food, so I joined others flocking to the local supermarket to stock up. The hospitals were trying to figure out how to still serve patients and not let visitors in the doors while none of us, including staff, were sure how safe we really were. While my doctor's appointments coincided with the greatest shut down this world has ever seen, I was faced with my own office not closing. For I was an essential worker in a hospital/clinic setting and all hands on deck were needed. There was no time for isolation and sorting out what was happening. Just as my homelife needed me, my work-life needed me even more. Many lives were at stake, not only physically, but also mentally and I was a psychotherapist. It was my privilege and my dedication. I had taken an oath, but no one really signed up for all of what we experienced.

So, my body kept going, but I felt disconnected. I knew mentally that I was fulfilling the role, but my mind and body were not really feeling anything. I experienced feeling alone, even though I knew there were people all around me. I saw how lost other people looked too. We were all going through the motions; together, but all silently suffering. I could feel souls screaming but there wasn't a single sound.

But that is not where this story ends. For this is a story of survival; a rebirth of the soul. It involves the sheer cry out of a system that is broken and needs revision. It is a story of getting knocked down and getting back up again. It is a story of sorting out stressors and conquering them one by one. It is a story of finding my breath again and of healing. I am happy to let you know that after two years of the fight, my brain tumor is stable, my autoimmune disorder reversed, the internal tremors have stopped, the numbness has gone from my feet, the google searching stopped. And those medication prescriptions... never filled.

It's also a story of never wanting anyone else to navigate this path alone like I had to. The old ways of coping with life stressors are not designed for the current complexity of today's world. That's why so many of us are falling apart at the seams. My life has now pivoted, and I understand the new mission I have been given. In everything, there is a lesson and I have been listening closely to mine. It now defines my purpose and gives meaning to why I was placed on this earth.

I have been helping patients, for the last 30 years, deal with anxiety and depression in a limited capacity as a local psychotherapist. It is now time to bring these gifts to a broader, very broken world that has lost its direction. A world currently spinning with no road map. No beginning or end. I hear the sounds of screaming souls. One's just like mine was not so long ago. We were never designed to navigate so many stressors alone. God has always had a plan for us, but we have lost our way. We've forgotten how to be still and listen. We've lost the community where we can be each other's company. We've lost our voices and souls along the way and it is time to get them back. It is time to rediscover you. It's time for Rest and Relaxation. The key is in self-care and I can show you the way.

You are not alone.

You were never alone.

WELCOME TO SELFCARE SOS BY MARCIA.

Self-care SOS by Marcia is designed to be a safe sisterhood of rest and relaxation where you can find the peace and joy needed to replenish and re-discover yourself. It includes group coaching, retreats, masterclasses and mentorships, helping you unwind from the craziness of the world, while getting you back on the path of physical and mental well-being. You can get all the updates by clicking on the below link, where you can choose the option of joining the International Self-Care Movement.

I wish you rest for your body, relaxation for your mind and peace for your soul. Forever in this together, Marcia

Https://linktr.ee/mdomecq

BUSINESS SPOTLIGHT

Lisa T. Daniel

Ready to confidently remove what is no longer serving you and walk through a spiritual transformation?

Lisa T. Daniel, is an author, speaker, television host, and a Heal Your Life® Teacher and Women's Empowerment Coach who is passionate about helping you discover a deeper, more insightful part of yourself as you radically and willingly shift out of hurt and brokenness and step into healing and gratitude.

Some call her a "Confidence Advocate" since she wholeheartedly seized the opportunity to work on self-reconstruction and energy-clearing, in order to admirably alter her life, attitude, and direction!

She attributes much of her success and growth to the teachings of Louise Hay. Because of this influence Lisa has since received numerous certifications, which she now uses in her thriving coaching practice. She empowers women to radically transform their life by combining the techniques of breath work, yoga, Pilates, Reiki, energy healing, and more.

Lisa works privately and conscientiously with her clients as they build unshakable confidence in a new and awakened life.

ARE YOU READY FOR YOUR SPIRITUAL JOURNEY?

Lisa will walk hand-in-hand with you on the personal experience of freeing your soul. You will begin to feel grounded and secure in your values and spiritual convictions, so you can live your highest and best life.

Join Lisa on a profound and pivotal journey of self-discovery and self-love and ultimately embrace the place where you feel abundant, hopeful and filled with purpose! She will help you naturally and bravely ascend into your highest spirituality.

Check out Lisa's other books, *Love Yourself Now* and *Yoga and Pilates for Your Mind, Body and Baby* as other free resources at https://theawakewoman.com/free-courses/

Begin your quest now for a spiritual awakening by enrolling in Lisa's 6-month course, "Awake Woman Academy". Receive $500 off when you enroll at https://theawakewoman.com/the-awake-woman-academy/.

Joni Goodman

This chapter is dedicated to Pat who was a mentor, sister-in-law, always by my side teaching me as together we cared for family. Pat always supported me, encouraged me to go for my goals. Teaching me how to be a Caregiver showing me what I lacked. Being her Caregiver was tough my heart says she was in peace to join our Angel family.

CHAOS TO BALANCE FOR PEACEFUL LIFE

Joni Goodman

Life is not a perfect schedule so prepare for the unexpected having a routine of balance can make life easier.

Waking up in the morning routine is set and in place to get my mindset and tone for the day ready. Before even getting out of bed say 3 positive statements. Some are: I chose to be focused and productive today. I chose positivity and calmness today. I chose to be present today. Change them now and then yet all are to set mindset and tone for the day to be positive and productive.

Life in 2012 was an unexpected turn for four of us in the family. We were in a car accident; one you see coming yet have zero way to avoid. Hubby did his best for least amount of impact. I have zero memories of the next nine hours. Just know from being told about what the accident was like; our van was totaled and the boys were seen and have concussions and other health related issues. Recovery started the following day as we all had rested and ready to face what we now had ahead of us. Follow ups became numerous due to concussions, bruising along with pain. For me I struggled for I was not there for the boys. Hubby handled all and did a great job. Through this all we needed to find a way to make our days as regular as possible. We needed to find out balance our routine. Having a son with Autism routine is a priority and all was taken away from the accident. We all started a journey to heal and find a way to put this all behind us. The boys, thankfully, were not part of the lawyer and conversations, the other insurance was tough and we never did go to court we settled for placing our boys on the stand to relive what they have healed and moved on from was not going to take place. Finally were back to a routine, family time and living life again. Sometimes you have to make choices over your mental health or proving a point; we opted to take mental health.

My follow up only added more negative news the tumor found in my brain in 2004 has changed becoming slightly larger. Memories were like wiped out gone no matter how hard I tried to recall past events just could not remember. As we all healed over time boys starting to return to school. They struggled for getting in a car was difficult at first. Teachers assisted them in returning and making accommodations for them to get back into school routine. See the accident occurred the day before school started so they were a tad late in starting the new year. Hearing how my brain has changed and my mind was worse than it had been prior all took a huge toll on all. We had to take time and slowly learn our new normal. I kept my updates and health quiet so boys could have a life not to worry on me. I found myself lost and confused how to live with no recall.

Moving forward we healed together and I searched out ways to heal and have memories to return to be whole again. I booked a discovery call with someone I had no idea who they were and honestly went into the call thinking yeah will try yet nothing has helped yet. Surprised for here is where major changes did start to occur. Through an exercise Kim was doing, a memory of my past was as clear as day. A memory from being 17 years old and dancing details were vivid and clear. That day I knew life had more in store for me and booked Kim to be my Coach and help me where medical could not. We worked together on learning and striving to be in the present in life to make a new balance.

Learning balance, self-care and being present in life took some major work and changes. Daily following the morning routine, blocking time for business, family fun time as well as setting strong goals felt like a new life unfolding. No longer focused on the disabilities or the I cannot activities. Change mindset and focus to the I can……. Having a fantastic doctor handle my brain was a huge comfort. She is so understanding and compassionate I was able to relax and understand how to focus on life and let my head do what it is going to do. Learned to take time for family, healing and doing what my mindset and body needed. Learned how to make time for healthy eating as well as block time for self-care. Focusing on taking care of you could be going for a walk; hanging out with friends; booking a camping trip; gardening. Find what recharges you and go for it.

Present all boys are adults following their goals and dreams. Each one of their path are unique fitting them where they are growing and succeeding. Reminding me they are grown it is time to make more me time doing what I enjoy. Felt time to drop the excuses while focusing on my business goals. A new chapter for us all really; them caring for many more life activities on their own and me having more open time. Active with a group of Entrepreneurs life was looking brighter each day. Enrolled in courses to be a Coach and NLP to help others. Focused on Caregivers for many are alone with no support. There are still bad days yet not months or years. Disabilities or health issues can truly take over your life if you do not take care of you; practice mindset and self-care regularly. You can do meditation; the above before you get up; leave your phone alone for first hour you are awake. Go to bed at the same time daily and wake up at the same time. So many ways for you to take care of you find what assists your mental health and wellbeing.

Here with Hubby being a Law Enforcement Officer many situations fell on me. See one of our sons has ADHD and one is high functioning Autism and one raised seeing Mom give much more care to the other two. Clearly balance was not well set back then. Honestly some days were hour by hour others routine and planned. Since balance was missing our youngest felt he was less than and did not matter. Felt I was not close to him and gave more attention to the others. While I cannot set the clock back we do talk and repair damage I caused due to lack of balance in life. More motivation to assist Caregivers so maybe one family can learn from my mistakes and not have a child in their teen years explain their feelings. Mistakes are part of life; how we fix the situation or handle is what makes the future. I opted to admit my mistake on how he felt due to my actions. In time I feel we can both move past our back and forth relationship and be very close.

As this chapter explains and shows I never focused on balance or schedules let alone set goals. Life here was a hot mess and truly took me a long time to notice. Hearing my youngest share how he feels was a major wake up call. We are working on a brighter future and heal becoming closer. Sadly never can I erase his younger years nor how he felt. Learn now to find your balance to avoid my errors.

Helping Caregivers in any situation is my passion. Being a Caregiver to many raising sons with special needs; assisting my sister-in-law Pat with family members taught me so much, from illness to mental health issues to end of life. Caregivers usually have their own personal life fad and focus on caring for other's needs. Living through this seeing how my youngest felt growing up never do I want any parent/Caregiver hear the words I did. Caregiving can be a short day or can be 24/7. Finding a balance along with help and support is truly a must. Set up your MUST do each day so no matter what you are taking care of yourself and your family.

Am still a Caregiver for loved ones each journey different and unique. Difference now is as I slip I push and set stronger goals; more self-care and most verify balance is there leaving no one feeling alone or unwanted. Make time for my own home and family so they are not ignored as in the past.

You can and will find balance; make it a priority most of all learn to ignore naysayers who say nonsense on your own path. Stop giving negative people and their comments any mind space. You are stronger; your goals are stronger. Set your balance to succeed your own goals. Take time as well to finding your strength healing you to strong mental health. This way someone's else's words bring negative will mean nothing at all. Chances are they will deny or never own up to their false statements and rumors that were untrue they told. Best to let it go and give them zero thought or mind space. You take control if they do come to reach out and talk to you do you want to or no? You do not have to hear them out or accept what they want to change now. Remember you are strong and have your own goals and balance to reach only you get to decide to hear them out and walk away.

Will you focus on balance so the tough negative times no longer knock you down and keep you down? All our family has been through I said enough! Today I wake up each day with goals and intention and trust me you can as well. You need to set your goals to the point where you get up with determination.

This is not a oh ok boom change process. You have to face and deal with past that you hid or avoided solving. You have to be open and admit your faults, not for the others yet for you. Many times you hear oh forgive will give you a second chance do not count on any of this do this for you and only you.

Today I still have slip ups as I am currently caring for a loved one. When they became sick I was like ok can handle this one. After all I cared for Pat and felt all was done correctly and she was well cared for so can do this one as well. As a family we came together and did hospice in our home. While I did not balance life to well we all worked together to care for Pat. One thing to note when you do in home hospice you only see a nurse once sometimes twice a day. Rest of the care is all on you. Having help and time to eat or rest is a much-needed aspect in your journey. One thing as a Caregiver know upfront no two cases are the same.

Few things to leave you with: each journey is different. Maybe reading mine sounds as if it was easy to solve and fix. Sadly that is not the case, youngest and I still are work in progress. There is not a day I cannot believe how as a Mom I missed his signs or did not see his pain. I was so unbalanced I focused on the two who had issues not all three equally. Take time when one you are a full time or part time Caregiver making sure you and your family life is balanced. Set block times to do activities, go see a movie or a hike whatever you all enjoy.

My hope is this chapter gives you examples of how if we have no balance life is harder. Finding joy, having friends can become impossible. One thing I have done is friendship is a two-way street. Second is if you tell me something follow through or trust declines in our friendship. These are my balance for who I hang with or socialize with, sometime walking away is tough yet in the long run worth it for your mental health.

If I can assist you in some way, please book a call with me. I would love to connect with you.

https://joni615.mybrandsystem.co/check-this-out?fbclid=IwAR0caSU-4laL5etHIMLjWxmXPQ6RnEcvSrKmvZFDOjNMDUCas6cgUQDH-Fz6s

Monika Greczek

My Dedication is to all my Mentors, Family, Friends, and Clients who continue to support me and keep me Shining! I LOVE you and I am so grateful for each one of you!

THE LIFE I DESIGNED

Monika Greczek

Ever since I could remember, I always had dreams and aspirations. I just never knew how it would ever come to life. All I heard from my parents was if you want something, get a job and work hard for it. Well, I couldn't wait to get a job and get the things I wanted. Again, no one told me how much it would cost and that there are taxes, etc.

I had no idea that this was going to prepare me for the future. There is no handbook on life. I think we all have this preconceived notion of how we'd life to turn out. Sometimes it falls into place, and sometimes there's a detour. What I do know, is it requires taking the first step into anything you choose to do, then following the steps until you have achieved whatever it is.

I knew I wanted to be a Cosmetologist and started looking for a school that I'd like to go to. I found the school and enrolled. I knew I wanted to be a receptionist at a Hair Salon to learn what goes on at the salon and how to take appointments and more. There were more things that I learned like closing out, inventory, talking to clients. These new techniques taught me the things I needed to succeed as a hairstylist. I knew after graduation I wanted to be a stylist at the salon I was working at, so I went to the owner and asked what I needed to do. He told me I was already doing it and as soon I receive my Cosmetology license I could start behind the chair. I was so excited, and at the same time, thinking it wasn't as hard as I thought it would be. It wasn't hard because I was already taking the steps and doing what was needed to move forward to achieve my goals, education, and job. I continued to learn, and loved that I was going to be a stylist at a well-known salon straight out of Cosmetology School.

Since, life doesn't come with a handbook, I knew that what I wanted to achieve came with steps to follow. Whether it's a class, project, goal, each has steps from start to finish. If you just follow those steps, you'll finish. If you miss steps, you'll just be taking detours or might wind up not finishing. I realized that if I set my intentions and followed through, I would accomplish it. If I did not, something would happen, or I just would forget about it. It was my choice to see things through and if I had questions or needed help, it was up to me to communicate what I needed.

I do this with everything in my life, and can totally agree that if I don't follow through, I would be upset with myself or never know how things would have turned out. Sometimes I write something down and then see if it important for me to do to.

Throughout this experience, I also asked my clients a lot of questions. I learned so much and took away many great things that came in handy throughout my life. I attracted many mentors and dear friends that shared much wisdom with me that helped me grow into the person I am today.

There are days where the thoughts in my head are running around like a hamster wheel. This sometimes makes me anxious and overwhelmed. I must realize what the next steps I have to choose are that will bring me closer to my goals. Then there are times I get scared or procrastinate on finishing things. I might get the nerve to finish and once again would tell myself that it wasn't as hard as I thought it would be. So, why don't I imagine that it's already accomplished, and everything is flowing with grace and ease? Why not do things with enthusiasm and see how it will all come together?

My days at the salon would flow. I loved my clients and couldn't wait for them to sit in my chair and put a smile on their faces. Just like starting my consultation with my clients, I asked what would they like to achieve with their hair during their visit? Once I got a clear picture of what they wanted I would start and finish their look by styling, cutting, coloring their hair to their desired look. If I missed any steps or didn't listen, then there would be mistakes and an unhappy clients. Thank goodness, I do my best listening, explaining, and following to achieve the desired results.

This prepared me to open my own salon and continue my goals and aspirations throughout my adult life. One thing I haven't mentioned yet, was that I was only 14 years-old and still in 8th grade when I started Cosmetology School and 21 years-old when I opened my salon.

All those things I learned I used in my everyday life with my family. I scheduled out my day and set my intentions and goals. After my son was born, I set intentions on the school I wanted him to attend to, things I wanted to teach him, places I wanted to show him, etc. I had a family and life goals. I also set intentions and goals with my husband and my home. If I was persistent and stayed on course, it all came to flourish. When I didn't have the passion or enthusiasm and didn't nourish my thoughts, things wouldn't come to life. It just like a flower, you plant the seed, water it, and when it grows, keep it nourished so it keeps in bloom. Plant the seed of your desires and goals, put it the steps to keep them growing and then watch them bloom.

I love the title of this book, *Life By Design*, and I blessed to be part of it. I didn't realize how much of my life was designed by my thoughts, goals, dreams, and aspirations. I am consistently creating the life I choose. Another great word is consistency. At first it may be hard, boring, or I may even doubt myself, but I keep following through because I know those steps I take will eventually turn into something. I became a great stylist because I was doing the same thing every day and getting better at it each day. I became the best mom I choose to be by doing the things a loving mom would do for her family. Each day, I repeat the steps that are involved in keeping my life moving forward. I continue to go to classes for continuing education, seminars for business owners, conventions for marketing, products, motivation, and more. It is up to me to do what I choose and what I want. People may have their opinions; they can have them if I don't allow them to affect me, because than I am doing something some else wants me to do. I have to ask myself if that will move me forward and help me with what I am doing or working on now? Unless I ask for an opinion or help because I need assistance to move forward.

I greet each day with love in my heart. Each morning, I set my intentions and say my affirmations, this gives me the foundation of my day and sets my happy mood. I also have a gratitude journal and do things with grace and ease. I have noticed that throughout these years, when I do things with LOVE and HAPPINESS, things get done, people around me are happy, I can feel the harmony all around me, and no one is complaining. Another thing I make sure I am conscious of each day is Love. Love for myself and everyone around me. Doing what I love never feels like work or a chore. Each day is a new and wonderful experience, and many wonderful things appear. I didn't understand when one of my client's said that it must be nice to do what I love. I had to think about that, and asked him if he loved what he was doing. He said no so I asked, "why not?" I proceeded to ask, if he didn't, why did he not look for another job that he would love and enjoy in the meantime? He said he never thought about that. He had put into his head that he had to do the job to support his family. He later came back with a big smile on his face and told me he has found a new job that he enjoyed and loved. He also said he couldn't believe that no one had had ever asked or shared what I had with him. The love I share with the people, family, clients, has rippled into many blessings and I am extremely grateful. I am doing things with love so that I can succeed in whatever I choose to do.

I am truly blessed that I control the story of my life and I am the creator of it. Have you taken the time to write your story? How does it start? What does it involve? How does it end? Or does it end? Maybe it's a legacy and moves on? Each day, I add to my story. I add more details, or something I see or hear sparks in my brain, and I must write it down, so I don't forget. I give it a lot of detail. It's like building a house, there are many details and things that need to be done before it is complete. What is it going to look like when it is complete? I work backwards from there and add all the people, things, supplies, and everything that goes along with it until I have all the details for whatever I am working on creating.

By doing this I have created and am still creating the person I love to be! I have also created a lovely salon and spa with wonderful, happy, loyal clients, products that work, and are healthy for our hair and body, an atmosphere that people feel happy, safe, and welcome. It is my second home, and since I spend many hours there, I want to be comfortable and make sure my clients are comfortable. I have created my home away from home, my happy place, where I go to retreat away from city life and recharge myself. I've always dreamed of having a log cabin where I would be at peace and just relax. I loved children and new I wanted to have one of my own. I knew what I wanted to name him. I could picture what he would be like and how he'd look as he grew, that was a dream that came true. He is now a handsome, intelligent, caring, and respectful teenager getting ready for college, and I can see how he is designing the life he wants. He is a lot more than that... I'd have to write another chapter. With all of that, it's what I first put into my mind, then picture, then write it all down, and start to create it into reality. What I focus on comes to flourish, good or bad. I am more mindful to focus on the positive and not feed into the negativity because I do not want it to come to the surface. It's like the saying "be careful what you wish for", the more your dwell on something, chances are it will come true.

I tested that theory and it taught me a lesson I had to climb out of. I felt like I was in quick sand and didn't see how I could get out of it. I had to change my mindset and know what I really wanted. I knew if I got myself into it, I could get myself out of it. Never will I allow negative self-talk to sabotage my dreams, thoughts, or goals. What we think is what we become.

For many years, I have envisioned what my holistic spa would look like. It has been a project. Each day I take the necessary steps to keep my vision and goal alive. Like Rome, it wasn't built in a day, this will all come together in its perfect timing. One of the things that I have always dreamed of, set my intentions, envisioned, and wrote down in detail was, was to have a log cabin, where I would be at peace and just relax. I envisioned it, put in all the details, and six years ago manifested it, exactly how I had envisioned it.

Now, at 51, looking back, I have taken some detours in life. I don't regret it, because it was all a learning experience and something to go through to get to the other side. There were many pauses that allowed me to be present with other things that occurred and needed my attention. I still own my salon 30 years later, and have transformed it to a holistic salon and spa. I am a mother, wife, sister, friend, and own two businesses.

I continue to take the steps I need to take care of my family, life, and business. Putting the steps together makes it easier for me to schedule my day to accomplish what I need to do.

I am sharing this with you and asking you to hold my intentions and seeing this come true, I believe that it takes a lot of energy and people to manifest big dreams and goals. This is my Press Release when my Holistic Spa opens!

MONIKA GRECZEK is a woman who has gone out and achieved her goals and continues to. She started to envision the life she wanted when she was a young girl. Through all the books, coaching, classes, education, work, and intentions, she has followed her dreams. She started doing hair at the age of 14, won 1st place in the manikin competition at the Cosmetology school she attended, then went on achieving all her goals, graduating top of her class. She received her Cosmetology License at 16 years of age and was promoted at the salon to assistant manager. Doing hair came naturally to her. Her clients loved the way they looked and felt after receiving services from Monika. Even now her clients love that they always feel better after their visit with her. She listens to herself and her clients and always does what is best. There are people from all over that come to see Monika and receive that magic though she has through doing hair, massage, body work, coaching, and engaging with them. She has become a fabulous hair artist, mentor, and coach.

She runs a World-renowned Holistic Spa, and has had the pleasure to travel to different parts of the world, Bali, Figi, Thailand, Italy, France, Poland, Varansi, India, Grindavik, Iceland, Healing Forests of Japan, Belize, Cape Town, South Africa, Mount Shasta, California, The Dead Sea, Austria, bringing her experience back and sharing it with everyone around her. Her spa is a gorgeous place to come to and receive treatments, services, shop, eat, relax, and more. The peaceful serenity is seen as you drive up to the beautiful Zen landscape with succulents, plants, flowers, rocks, and fountains. You feel like you are in one of these amazing places that she has visited and brought back with her to share the beautiful experiences with others.

Monika is invited to speak all over the world and share her knowledge. She has continued to grow into this World-renowned Holistic Spa. She started learning about essential oils after she graduated Massage Therapy School and started sharing the benefits of massages and oils with her hair clients. They learned how to take better care of themselves and she knows she wanted it to grow into something more. It became her passion to learn more things about the body and mind, how to help people that didn't know how to start helping themselves. It was her passion, enthusiasm, spirit, and determination to create a place a life that feels joyful, full of spirit, energy, and enthusiasm each day.

She sees the blessings that have been bestowed on her through all the things she has shared with everyone around her. Her family is grateful for everything she has taught them and shared with them to become a wonderful family unit. It is truly a gift to enjoy the wonderful things that are a part of her life and all the things that keep flowing into her life.

She has had the honor to speak and teach at Hay House' Heal Your Life Workshop, be interviewed by Deepak Chopra, meet Shamans from all over the world who come and do retreats at her spa. Famous people also come to her to connect with themselves and receive the exquisite treatments the spa has to offer.

Her family was a delight to meet and be around, they shared food, stories, and all the phenomenal things they have discovered through Monika's sharing. They are a part of her legacy, and she is grateful that they are living their lives to the fullest.

Monika enjoys starting her day with prayer, mediation, and reading. Then setting her intentions for the day and going out and manifesting those intentions.

Monika truly loves what she is doing. I see the happiness, love, enthusiasm in her and she welcomes everyone as if she knew them all her life.

I interviewed Monika in her Log Cabin home; this place is breathtaking. I understand why she loves spending time with her son and husband here. It is an oasis of tranquility, peace, and love. I felt it as soon as I walked in. Monika is living the life she always dreamed of a life that was filled with peace, love, joy, passion, creativity, spirituality, and prosperity. She is living the life that she has manifested and dreamed of.

Why do I choose the Holistic approach? As a young woman, no one ever educated me on the chemicals that are found in hair, body, and facial products (make-up included). Throughout the years, I have had clients that suffer from smells, allergies, diseases, and more. While talking with them, I discovered they were never taught about products either. Well, those products get absorbed into your body and in the long run can cause damage and even cancer. I strive to use products that do not have hormone disrupters, and are toxic free, organic, therapeutic and healthy for your over-all wellbeing. I also share more of my favorite products at the https://monikag.mybrandsystem.co/virtual-spa-experience/

Tina Guimar

This chapter is dedicated to my granddaughter, Mariella. May you always have the confidence to follow your heart, chase your dreams, and live life to the fullest. I love you with all my heart.

ALIGNING WITH YOUR HIGHER PURPOSE

Tina Guimar

We've all experienced moments in our lives where we feel trapped or out of sorts with our current situation. Whether it be unhappiness at work, feeling stuck in a stagnant relationship, or being caught up in the fast pace of modern life, searching for more peace and satisfaction can often seem impossible.

But what if there was another way? Deep soul searching and aligning with your higher self are powerful tools to help you find clarity, focus on what is truly important to you, and rediscover your core being - your true identity. By taking a moment to quiet the outer noise of life's responsibilities and pressures, we can begin an inner journey that will ultimately allow us to see ourselves with newfound confidence, adjusted perspectives and rekindled passion.

I invite you to come explore this journey with me today as I discuss how discovering yourself through deep soul searching and connecting to your higher self can lead you back onto the path meant just for you! This exploration will involve connecting to your higher self: the part of yourself that is intuitive, powerful and strong. The benefits of engaging in this process can lead to more clarity about decisions, peace in moments of uncertainty and a greater sense of connection and understanding.

If you are anything like me, you tend to put everyone and everything else first. Before you can restore balance between anything, you have to focus on who YOU are without anyone or anything else. It takes a little work to do this deep soul searching and to understand who you truly are - who you have the potential to be – but my goal today is to make this process easier for you. When you become aligned with your true purpose and passion (your higher self), you will feel fulfilled and in a state of flow - then nothing feels like a chore.

Prior to 2015, I was living the dream... or shall I say what I thought was living the dream. Great career, family, house, college degrees, and a schedule that ate up all the hours in the day with no time or energy at the end of the day. You know? All the things we are told are important to be successful. The only thing that came out of this lifestyle I created up until then was feeling exhausted and miserable. I found myself complaining all the time which only allowed the negativity to take over, bad things to happen and relationships to deteriorate.

On Easter 2015, we lost our home and all of our belongings in a house fire. While struggling through the rebuild of our house, working full time, attending school part-time and taking care of my family, I was determined to continue to meet all the goals I set out to accomplish even though more and more bad things kept happening. I felt like there was a huge dark cloud over my head that would not go away.

I finished school and earned my master's in business administration degree (MBA), but I found myself burnt out, more exhausted and more miserable than ever before. That was the first turning point where I realized there was more to life than working ALL THE TIME! I had been at my job for 10 years and finally made the decision to start setting boundaries. I longed for that work-life balance that people talked about.

When I still couldn't find that balance at the job I had been at for 10 years, I decided it was time to find a new job. A change would be good, right? I went from a fast paced, work all the time environment to a very laid back, no cares in the world environment. Culture shock set in! I began to change who I was to "fit in" with the new work culture. This became very frustrating to me but I pushed through because I was resilient. After all, this is the life I was supposed to be living.

After only a few months in this new job, we had 3 major deaths in the family. Little did I know, my second turning point would come on February 5, 2017, the day we lost my brother to suicide. I was devastated and wondered when I would wake up from this nightmare. I became very angry and isolated. I decided it was time to stop being so proud and seek help. That is when I started on this journey of self-discovery and deep soul searching. I didn't realize it at the time but I was lost—I didn't know who I was anymore or why I was supposed to be here on this earth. What I did know was that I had to change something because I could not continue down this miserable path any longer.

I was fortunate to receive many tools and techniques that have helped me to discover who I am and what I am meant to be doing, essentially restoring the balance and serenity that I so longed for. To be really happy doing what I love and not just having to go through the motions every day. When I started implementing the tips I am about to give you, my stress and anxiety were reduced, my depression was eliminated and I was able to clear my head so I can focus on what was best for my family and me. That is the power of living in the present moment—also known as mindfulness.

One of the things that was pointed out to me in the early stages of this new journey was, "if you are trying to change who you are, then you are in the wrong place" and wow, did that hit home. Up until then, I was molding myself to fit in everywhere I turned instead of just being the real me. Have you ever felt like that? The real question is, do you really know who you are and what you are meant to do? Stick with me as I give you some of the things that helped me turn my life around for the better and create a balanced and fulfilled life.

The very first thing I want to share with you is to practice gratitude daily. Practicing gratitude is a fantastic way to attract more positivity into your life. It's amazing how appreciating what you already have can open up powerful opportunities for even greater success and joy. By tuning into the good things in your life, such as close relationships and meaningful work, you can recognize how fortunate you are and be happy with everything that comes your way. Gratitude also has been linked to improved mental health, increased resilience, and better overall well-being. Whether it's jotting down three or five things you're grateful for each day before going to bed or writing thank-you notes to those who have helped you in life, finding new ways of expressing gratitude every day will absolutely have a positive effect on your world.

Number two is visualization. Visualization is a powerful skill that can help us to achieve our goals no matter how big or small. It's the ability to turn a goal into an achievable reality, allowing us to feel as if it has already been accomplished. When we visualize something with clarity and consistency, it helps put us in a headspace where we can actively work towards achieving that dream. Visualizing is a great way to ensure success as it encourages optimism and a focus on solutions rather than problems, enabling us to set achievable milestones towards our desired target. With commitment and consistency when visualizing, plus taking actionable steps towards our dreams, anything is possible! So, if you have ambitions for yourself, don't forget to take some time for visualization each day - you never know what your mind may be capable of achieving!

The third thing that helped me is mediation. Meditating is such a powerful practice with deep and long-lasting effects—you can feel the benefit almost immediately. Each time you clear your mind and embrace your inner stillness, you're planting a seed for enhancing every part of your life. It helps to improve energy levels, reduce stress, improve sleep patterns and more. Meditation can even help to build healthy coping habits and give rise to feelings of joy and empathy. If that wasn't enough, it can also increase positivity towards yourself, allowing you to raise above any self-doubt issues. So, if you have the time, even just for 5 minutes, why don't you take the opportunity today to just pause and appreciate the power of meditation!

Now, if you're feeling a bit stuck in life, or lacking direction and purpose, it's time to get digging into what it truly means to be you. It can feel overwhelming trying to figure out one's identity and place in the world, but with a little guidance and persistence it can be a fulfilling journey of self-discovery. To help yourself along, start by making a list of your core values – those things that are important to **YOU** and guide the decisions you make. From there, take some time for deep reflection by journaling – letting yourself become aware of your own beliefs, thoughts and feelings. Finally, build plans around how to put those values into action in order to live a meaningful life that is just right for you. You will be well on your way to aligning with your higher self.

We all have something special to contribute to this world. Life is an opportunity for you to discover what it is that really lights you up and brings you joy; if we align with our higher purpose, then the journey can truly be magical. Identifying what your life purpose is can take some time, but by reflecting on moments when you've felt fulfilled or most alive, this will quickly give clues towards what you should be striving for each and every day. Having a greater passion and purpose to strive towards can make all of your actions aligned and focused – leading to achieving even bigger results in turn. Make sure that wherever you're heading has a sense of meaning and excitement, because it won't feel like mastering a chore, but rather an adventure worth pursuing!

What I want to leave you with today, based on my experience, is this: set aside everything you have learned up until now, make sure you are doing what you love, take time for yourself and your loved ones, be present as much as possible, always be authentic, follow your heart and chase your dreams. Times can be challenging, but if you remain focused and keep moving forward, you will find your balance and alignment. Time is going to pass anyway. All you need to do is make a choice and put that choice into take action. Be open to new ideas, be ready to transform your life, and learn to embrace change. Listen to the little nudge that is telling you that you are made for more. Have patience with yourself. You are worth it! The sky is not the limit... the only limits are the ones we place on ourselves.

If you have been feeling trapped or out of sorts with your current situation, I would love for you to take advantage of some of the tools and resources I put together to help you align to your higher self faster. Just visit tina-guimar.com or scan the code at the beginning of this chapter to access these powerful tools so you can step back into your power and become who you are meant to be. Your family and your future self will thank you.

Sharon Keathley

So much appreciation and gratitude to my sweet husband, Jack, who has forever encouraged me to Dream Big and Never Quit!

ALLOW YOUR PASSION TO OVERRULE YOUR FEAR

Sharon Keathley

"I'm too old!"

"I don't know anything about running a business!"

"I don't have enough experience!"

"I don't have enough time."

"I'm not tech-savvy!"

I have heard it all before (I've actually said those very phrases!) and it's all just a bunch of hogwash! It's your fear speaking. If you recognize that people have problems, and you have a passion to help those people solve their problems, and you have the solution to help them do it, then you have what it takes to turn that passion into a profitable business. It's never too early and it is certainly never too late. You will always have an element of fear. You will always be learning. You will never know everything, but you have more than enough knowledge, right now, to build your dream business. It's been my experience that passion trumps age, determination trumps lack of knowledge, and the willingness to learn trumps everything else.

Like so many of us, my life hasn't been easy. I grew up a welfare kid, the youngest of five, actually ten, including my stepbrothers who were grown by the time I arrived. I barely remember my dad; he was sixty-two when I was born and had a lot of health issues. My mom worked and struggled to keep things going. My sisters raised me.

I knew we were different, but it was years before I realized how much my mom and older siblings protected me from all the struggles. I was spoiled by my whole family, spoiled in a good way. I was a good kid. I loved school and excelled. We didn't have extras, but Mom made sure I had everything I needed for school, even if that meant the family as a whole struggled. I was in junior high before I realized how spoiled I really was. This made me work even harder. I found odd jobs to pay for extras, like cheerleading shoes.

My only brother was injured, paralyzed from a cervical fracture sustained in a fall, when I was still in junior high. He spent months in a rehab hospital, then was released home. By that time, my sisters were married and no longer lived at home. The care he required added an even bigger burden on my mom. She never complained, we just made it work. I became the driver in the family, transporting my brother to and from doctors appointments and helped my mom care for him. That is likely where I developed my love of nursing.

Because of my mom's support, I received a college scholarship which allowed me to be the first person in my family to be able to go to college. I selected a nearby college and was home every weekend to help my mom.

I've now been a nurse for over forty-five years. I graduated on a Friday and, wasting no time, I went to work as an operating room nurse the following Monday. I loved every minute I spent in that operating room for the next ten years. But, you know, there was not a single course in nursing school geared toward running a business. We were taught chemistry, anatomy, patient care, and bedside nursing. But in the years of practicing in the medical profession, (likely, it's the same in your profession) one cannot help but pick up many skills along the way that prepares one for the business world, without even being aware that you are being prepared. The skills for prioritizing, scheduling, workflow, cost-effectiveness, outcomes, etc. were ingrained over the years.

Most of all, I learned compassion, empathy, kindness, generosity, dependability, and understanding. I learned communication skills, integrity, the skills of persuasion, self-awareness, troubleshooting, team building, and so many other leadership skills. If you have worked with others, you probably also learned some of these skills and maybe more. You just may not have realized that those are exactly the skills needed to step into the world of business and be the phenomenal leader we all know you can be!

I worked hard, loved the jobs I had, and worked my way into management positions. I had some wonderful bosses and some not-so-great ones, but my idea of doing a great job didn't always coincide with management's ideas. Sometimes it's not good to rock the boat, especially if you aren't in control of that boat.

I left bedside nursing and was working for a company providing consulting services for insurance companies. The company had a completely different outlook on what constituted success than I did. Yeah, maybe I was a bit of a rebel and maybe I still am. I believed there was more. A profession shouldn't just be about going to work, coming home, and repeating the process for the next fifty years. I wanted to make a real difference in the lives of the patients I served. I began to wonder what I would do differently if I could run the business my way.

I began putting ideas together and approached an insurance company with my plan. I had actually developed a business plan and didn't even know it. They liked the plan! I was told if I could pull something like that together, they would be my first client. I was over forty years old. I was newly divorced. My oldest child struggled with drug addiction and was constantly in and out of jail, mostly in. My youngest had just graduated high school and was headed for college. Both of us were trying to find our way in a world of uncertainty, unsure from day to day what the next day would hold.

I had big ideas, but I also had low self-esteem, a lack of self-confidence, and a failed marriage. I struggled as a mother, not knowing how to help my youngest deal with having an older sibling in and out of prison and having to cope with the aftermath of a school shooting. The pain of living through such a horrific event never goes away. Counseling helped some, but when one's world is turned completely upside down, that shock is not forgotten, even with time. We still honor that day and always will.

I worried about so many things. I had a good income. I had insurance, I had a 401K. This probably wasn't the best time to jump ship and start a business. I had no experience. I knew nothing about building a business. I had no idea whether or not I could make it happen. The truth was, I was afraid to take the leap.

Then I remembered everything my family had given up for me. To do nothing at this point just didn't feel right. I wasn't raised that way. I could do more. So, instead of looking for excuses, I looked for reasons why I should start my own company. I was good at what I did. I had a great idea and already had the support of a huge company if I decided to pursue it. The truth was, both my kids were adults. They didn't need me in that way anymore, I was just using that as an excuse. I needed to do this. So, in 2003, I started my own medical consulting company.

We can find so many excuses. We can convince ourselves of so many reasons not to pursue our passion. But if we allow our passion to overrule our fears and have a plan in place, there is no reason why passion cannot take us to the top! Life is all about balance. How do you balance your dreams and your passion with your responsibilities and obligations when there may be a huge gap between them? You may have to work harder and do things others won't do to be able to achieve what others never will. You may need more time to accomplish your goals. You may need to learn how to schedule your time more efficiently. You may need to learn to delegate a little more often. You will want to involve your family with what you are doing. You may need to learn how to say no to some things that are not serving you and your family. I decided to let my passion rule.

Assuming you have that passion, I would like to share three things I was willing to do that allowed me to develop and grow my business into a six-figure business the very first year (this was back in 2003!).

I WAS WILLING TO LEARN

When I say I knew nothing about owning or running a business, I mean I knew absolutely nothing about it. But I was willing and eager to learn. I found business leaders willing to mentor me. I talked with other business owners, asked questions, listened to their advice, developed more questions, interviewed more business owners, and made lists of things they mentioned as "must-haves." For three months, I enrolled in every business class the Small Business Association offered (no online classes back then!). I learned how to write a real business plan, use spreadsheets, do some quick accounting, learned enough about taxes to form a Corporation and even learned Quick Books. I worked my job hard and saved every penny I could for a cushion.

I WAS WILLING TO INVEST IN MYSELF

No one is an island and neither are you or your business. Solopreneurs are awesome. I have been one my whole adult life, but I can't say that I built my business entirely by myself. I had so much help along the way. I have, however, invested in myself in a couple of different ways. My best investment was a mentor, a coach. I didn't have time or money to waste stumbling through the unknown. I was honest with myself about my shortcomings and worked on ways to improve those.

I'm an introvert by nature, but I stepped out of my comfort zone and attended the Chamber meetings and other local business meetings. I got more involved in the community. I learned early that networking was important, even if it made me uncomfortable. I practiced my elevator pitch and honed it to perfection. I took inventory of what was working for me, as well as the areas where I was lacking, and focused on improving those areas. I borrowed books and video tapes from the library for motivation and to improve my self-confidence. I attended business seminars. I meditated long before that was a big thing. I knew if I was going to succeed, my head had to be right. Today that is called mindset.

I WAS WILLING TO WORK

I took the advice I received from my mentor, the videos, the books, and the professional trainings, and put all that advice into action. Some people believe you have to have everything in place before you should start a business, but I can tell you that you don't. Some people are in the "learning mode" for way too long. Don't do that. You already know everything you need to know to get started. Learn a new skill and implement it, tweak it, and move on. Skills are built upon each other. If you never implement the first skill, then your foundation is not solid enough to support the next skill. You'll end up overwhelmed with information and nothing to show for it.

I have never regretted stepping out of my comfort zone twenty-plus years ago. It was scary and yes, there were times I wasn't sure I would make it. I met every challenge just as I did the first step and let my passion for helping my patients overrule my fear. My kids were proud of their momma, and I was proud to be able to be an example for them that you can do anything if you have the passion to overcome your fears.

You might say well, yes, all that may have worked for me back then, but what about now? We are in the digital world now, a world where you have to show up online, in video. Technology is a must if you are planning to build an online business. And I would say, yes it is, but use that to your advantage. To have an online business, especially one based on social selling, you really must have an online presence. But you don't have to be an influencer on every social platform. Pick one and get started (Facebook and YouTube are two of the most common, but Instagram, TikTok, and even Pinterest work for many people).

In my opinion, what you must have in today's world to succeed with an online business is the passion to help others and the solution to help someone solve a problem. If you have that passion, the rest can be developed. It's a learning process, but some things don't change. You still have to be willing to learn, willing to invest in yourself, and willing to work.

Thankfully, now, there is a process that is simple to follow, a process that will allow your business to generate income quickly. There is help available to walk you through that process and there is no reason you cannot accomplish your dreams and allow your passion and your solution to help others while you grow the business you have been wanting to build. If you are ready to get started or if you are struggling with growing your online business, I would love to be your mentor. Reach out and let's walk through that process. You just need to allow your passion to overrule your fear!

info@easystuff360.com
www.easystuff360.com
www.sharonkeathley.com
Facebook
https://calendly.com/easystuff360

BUSINESS SPOTLIGHT

Laura Cooke

KEEPING BALANCED: SETTING AND HOLDING BOUNDARIES

Do you say yes, when you mean no? Do you take on more than you can handle? Do you end up feeling depleted, exhausted and maybe even a little resentful?

You're not alone! We are taught to help others, put ourselves last and do as much as we can in the time we are given. But guess what? If our cup is not full, we have no business to try and fill someone else's.

Boundaries are compassionate ways we can take care of ourselves. No one who loves or respects us would disrespect our boundaries.

When we say no, not now, or I'm sorry I can't, we give ourselves what we need to restore, refill, and then reach out when we have the time and energy to fully show up for that person.

When we say yes when we don't have the bandwidth to help, we end up irritable, resentful, and tapped out.

We often feel that setting and holding boundaries feels "mean" or that it might do damage to the relationship but I'll ask you – which is kinder? Saying yes and being short, dismissive, irritated, and clearly annoyed or saying no and then being fully present, prepared, and patient when we DO have the time and energy?

If you asked someone to help you would you prefer they say "I can't right now but I do have time tomorrow afternoon"? Or would you like them to give you that sly grin that says "Fine... .but I don't want to and you will pay for this one way or another eventually"?

I know I'm using drastic examples, but even little micro aggressions cause damage as they add up over time.

Do you need the tools and language to set better boundaries? Scan the code above for access to my Free Masterclass which comes with a self-study video, worksheet and setting boundaries checklist.

It's time to make time for you. It's kinder to say no or not now. No one wins when you don't have the time or energy to fully show up for something or someone.

Make "No" your word of the year. It's a full sentence and those who love and respect you will appreciate your honesty.

Sherril Porterfield

This book is dedicated to my husband Jim and my daughter Caroline who have given me amazing love and support over the past 10 years. Without them I would not be where I am today. They have been my encouragers, cheerleaders, and at times caregivers who always saw my potential, even on days I was ready to give up. I'm grateful for both of you every day.

BEING A STAY-AT-HOME MOM IS *NOT* WHAT I SIGNED UP FOR

Sherril Porterfield

With both of us in high pressure jobs that required frequent travel, my husband and I were professionals at making sure the other one was "on the ground" before heading out of town. We created the ultimate tag team to ensure someone was home to pick up our daughter from school before "late stay" closed for the afternoon.

Having no other family nearby to help out, we juggled our travel and careers, somehow always making it work. We were often like ships passing in the night, always making sure that one of us was home to care for our daughter.

I set high standards for myself, always striving for perfection. You see, being "super mom" was important if you were not always home. I didn't realize then how much my life revolved around "making up" for lost time. Weeks that my husband and I were both home were extra special, and we lived for the weekend when we could enjoy time together as a family.

As the queen of multitasking, "The busier the better" was my motto. Becoming a healthcare consultant was the highlight of my career as a Registered Nurse. Since this was my dream job, my husband and I committed to making our crazy travel schedules work. This was how we rolled.

We kept up this frantic, fast pace lifestyle for over five years. When my daughter reached elementary school, I began to feel guilty when I missed school activities. Because of this guilt, I started putting extra stress and pressure on myself. I found myself caught up in the mindset that everything I did had to be "Pinterest-worthy" and over the top. Spending long nights testing my creative boundaries only made matters worse. But since I was missing out on Caroline's activities, I thought… why not show the stay-at-home moms what this working mom could do.

It wasn't until I hit a major bump in the road that I realized how out of balance my life really was. While out to dinner on a Saturday evening, my "perfect" life came crashing to a halt. What started as a quiet family dinner at a favorite restaurant turned into my worst nightmare. Bizarrely, a heavy lantern fell from a high shelf and hit me on the head. Who knew that the lantern was unsecured, and that the badly behaved child behind me would "knock" it loose by beating on the wall. I saw stars and was momentarily unconscious. All I knew was that we had created a scene and that I had the worst headache ever.

With the urgent care closed, I told my husband to take me home so I could put ice on my head.. (My husband always has said that nurses are the worst patients.) When I started vomiting a couple of hours later, my husband took me to the emergency room. They performed a CT scan, examined me, and said to go home and take it easy–that it was a minor concussion and everything would be okay in a few days. What initially presented as a minor concussion turned out to be a traumatic brain injury that had severe lasting effects.

Little things I took for granted each day were a struggle. Just getting out of bed and getting dressed was a challenge. Having my eight-year-old daughter help me to the bathroom was a lesson in humility. Not being able to take care of myself or my family became my new normal. Losing my job was nothing compared to the feelings of loss I was experiencing by losing my independence. What good was a Master's Degree when you can't help your third grader with her math homework?

Days carried over to months. When the chronic headache, frequent migraines, balance issues, and memory issues did not resolve, realization finally set in. I didn't know how long these issues would last, but I knew I would never work as a nurse again. How could this be happening to me?

The day I realized I would permanently be a stay-at-home mom was traumatic. I cried, I shouted, I threw some things. This was not anything I had ever wanted, and definitely was not in my plan.

What made this terrible situation worse was that I found myself as a stay-at-home mom who couldn't do what it took to run a household. I was stuck at home, dealing with chronic pain, struggling to hold it together in foreign territory. To say I was angry and depressed was an understatement. My career was my identity. What was I supposed to do now? If I had to be a stay-at-home mom, I didn't have to like it.

After a couple years of living in this nightmare of chronic pain and brain injury issues, I was frustrated and angry about being stuck in such a dark place. I knew that despite all the symptoms and pain I was experiencing, things had to change. Whatever it took, I needed to get my life back.

Through therapy, determination, and a lot of prayer, my outlook started to improve. My computer skills were still problematic, but an occupational therapist encouraged me to "go live" on Facebook as a way to help my speech and memory issues improve. Public speaking at meetings or conferences was never challenging for me, but thoughts of "going live" on Facebook terrified me. That first live video was rough, but each video became easier. My memory slowly improved, and over time, it was easier to speak the words I wanted to say.

By focusing on my faith and gratitude, my outlook also significantly improved. I realized that there were a lot of people in worse situations than mine. I was blessed with a supportive family who loved me unconditionally.

One day the realization hit me. What I had viewed as the worst thing that could have ever happened was actually a blessing. I was now able to spend time with my family and enjoy the precious gift of time with my husband and daughter. There are so many things in life I would have missed out on if I were still running the corporate rat race.

It took tragedy and loss to allow me to see how out of balance my life really was. This injury gave me a new lease on life. My current life was not what I had pictured, but my life allowed me to enjoy things I would have never experienced without this bump in the road.

Over time, I have been able to find a way to work from home as my physical limitations allow. I have been blessed to be able to encourage other women who have experienced tragedy and loss to help make their dreams a reality.

Looking back, I had no idea that the balancing act we lived each week was not normal. I had no idea how out of balance and out of control things really were.

God has turned my tragedy into a blessing that I am able to use to encourage others. A morning routine, setting boundaries, putting family first, and a grateful heart have all made my life better. Today, I have found a balance between my life, work, and family that allows me to enjoy life like I never thought possible. Each day is a gift, and I embrace it with gratitude.

The mission of Sherril & Tonia Coaching is to help online marketers create a solid content-to-sales conversion system that will allow them the freedom to live the life of their dreams, doing what they love…in work or play.

My business partner Tonia and I would love for you to join our FB group, *Social Media Marketing Made Simple and Fun*. Click the link below for **DETAILS**, as well as a **ROADMAP** that shows you the 7 daily **ACTION STEPS** you can take today to get Leads, Engagement & Sales.

https://members.sporterfield.com/roadmap-funnel-for-freebie

Dara Lee Simmons

I dedicate this chapter to my two children, Sean and Kayla Renee, who witnessed first-hand the juggling act of a busy mom who didn't always get it right, but in their own time, have both become outstanding, kind, honest, loving, and productive adults.

EAT, PLAY, ACTION

Dara Lee Simmons

Let me ask you this question: Why do you seek balance in your work, play and family life? You may think the answer is obvious, but truly this is different for everyone. I believe the answer to this must come first, before you can learn how to achieve balance. Then, what do you do once you find that balance? I'm here to share my insights on this process and offer tips that have helped me over the years.

Let's start with a little bit about me. I've worked my entire career supporting and teaching both adults and children with disabilities, which was truly a career of passion. I really loved what I did and strived to make the most positive impacts wherever I could.

In addition to my career, I was married, had two children, parents and siblings nearby, and wove additional schooling as well as a side business into my life all while trying to remain sane. First question, why did I have so many things on my plate? Because it's who I am destined to be, a woman with a purpose, passion, and plateful of to-do's.

Today, I'm retired from my traditional career, yet I continue to keep my plate full because I want to make the most out of life, and I'm far from done impacting lives. I've touched hundreds, but my goal is to touch thousands.

Ok, enough about me. What about you. Why do you seek balance? Is it because you feel overwhelmed? Stressed? Is your work load impacting your health? Do you feel guilty because you can't get everything on your to do list done? Are you getting grouchy? Do you feel isolated from the world because you are so busy? Is your house a mess? Are your relationships suffering?

If one or more of these are affecting you, then I have some answers for you. First, take a deep breath. Good, now one more. Hear me... you are not alone. At some point we all have these feelings, especially in today's fast paced world, when we are being pulled in multiple directions, it's easy to go, go, go, and forget to stop and breath. So, please remember to stop, and breath.

Balancing the many facets of our lives takes practice and often help from others. Others who have been there before you or right alongside you. I'm still working to keep things balanced, and honestly, some days are much better than others. It's ok if we don't get it right every day, because we will never get it right every single day, that's simply not humanly possible. What we strive for is to get it almost right one day and build on that. And some days, we will totally fall apart and get almost nothing done, but that's ok because we will get a fresh start tomorrow.

I believe the **TWO BIGGEST CONTRIBUTORS** to keeping me balanced all these years have been eating a "mostly" healthy diet and making sure I made time for my own leisure. I realize this may sound counter intuitive, taking time to eat healthy and "play time" for myself when I barely have time to do what I already have on my plate. Please read on and let me explain.

FIRST, A HEALTHY DIET DOES NOT NEED TO BE COMPLICATED OR TIME CONSUMING, especially with the options we have available to us today. You can choose one of the many home delivery options available, or learn from me how to eat good food, real fast. Personally, I eat a whole foods, plant-based diet, most of the time, but this by no means needs to be your path. However, eating more plant foods, and less highly processed foods can only help you. Avoiding added sugars, fats, preservatives, and artificial colors and sweeteners is sure to have a positive impact on your health and energy. If you do decide to choose a more whole foods, plant-based diet, I promise you that you will have more energy, more stamina, and overall better health so that you can tackle the multiple things on your agenda.

Let me explain in a little more detail. Plant foods; fruits, vegetables, beans, and nuts are full of vitamins, minerals, fiber and are plentiful in variety. And I get that it may sound overwhelming to begin down this path, but trust me, it doesn't have to be.

First, begin by adding more fresh fruits and vegetables to your current daily routine. Maybe add berries to your cereal or veggies to your eggs in the morning. Replace the breakfast meat with a piece of fruit. I have many more free ideas available for you at the end of the chapter be sure to follow my link.

Switch out sodas and other sweetened drinks for water. Just plain water, or add sliced fruit such as lemons, limes, or oranges; believe it or not, even cucumber slices add a nice fresh flavor to water.

Adding beans, sprouts, nuts, seeds, and grains to your salads along with a variety of greens creates a heartier and more enticing meal. Fruits such as apples, oranges, and pears can be sliced to add a whole new dimension to your salad.

If you are interested in learning more about either how to get creative with eating more plants, or if you are like me and want to jump all in, there are a ton of great plant-based pod casts, cookbooks, and websites. A website I would highly recommendation is forksoverknives.com. There's a beginner's guide as well as recipes and a great informative film to be found.

SECONDLY, ARE YOU TAKING TIME FOR YOURSELF? Are you kidding me you say!! I can barely squeeze in all the millions of things I'm already doing for my job, my family, my mate, my household, and I even have a side gig I'm pursuing; and you ask if I'm taking time for me?

I know this sounds counter intuitive, but hear me out. We must, I repeat must, take care of ourselves. Our inner souls, our engines that make us tick, and tick, and tick all day long must be nurtured. If we do not fuel this inner most precious piece of ourselves, we will eventually run out of steam. That's the why, and I'm about to show you the how.

Remember when you were a kid? What did you do all day, every day? You played right? Kids learn so many lessons by playing, how to follow rules, how to take turns, how to be creative, how to take risks, basically they learn how to be kids.

As adults, spending time playing, or engaged in leisure activities, brings us back to connect with ourselves. After all, we are the most important person in our lives. Without ourselves, we are no one.

It's kind of like the oxygen on the airplane, the instruction is always to give yourself oxygen first, then help those in your care. Why is this? Because if you are not saved, you can't possibly help save someone else.

It does not matter what you do for your leisure, but it really should be something that relaxes and stimulates you at the same time. Now, personally, I'm not a big fan of TV, but that's a story for another day. With that said, if your favorite leisure time activity is to sit down and watch a good Hallmark movie, then by all means indulge in that; but please do yourself a favor and be fully engaged. If you are folding laundry or creating your meal and grocery list for the week while watching, you are not fully recharging your own battery.

Curling up with a good book, alone and away from distractions for 30 minutes will do your body good. Taking a walk in the woods or around the block can rejuvenate your soul. Take up a sport, yoga, tennis, golf or pickle ball and get it into your schedule once a week. The amount of recharging and reenergizing you get will far exceed the two hours of productivity time you lost.

Maybe you prefer crafting or visiting friends or having a date night with your significant other. Whatever it is that takes your mind off the daily grind, do yourself a favor and make it happen. You will thank me for this one day.

If you take these two activities, eat healthy and allow yourself some play time, you will without a doubt see your energy increase and you will enjoy a burst of productivity as well. With more energy and better focus, all the other time management and balancing strategies you have will become even more effective.

To find more helpful tips on starting your day with super simple plant-based breakfast meals, or to benefit from my favorite site where I get help to prepare good food real fast or to follow my blog, please check out my link below. I hope to see you soon.

www.achievewithdaralee.com

Peace and Love,
Dara Lee Simmons

Tonia Smith

This chapter is dedicated to my daughter Ashley whose strength and courage continue to awe me. My husband Rick was my boyfriend during this time and still is my rock. To my granddaughter Alaina who came into this world changing all of our lives for the better.

MOM, I'M PREGNANT...
PLEASE, DON'T BE MAD

Tonia Smith

Ever look back at that one pivotal moment in life, where destiny could have been changed forever....if only you had made a different choice?

It's been 25 years now. I can still remember waking up and quickly "hushing" my dogs who woke me up with their barking in the middle of the night. I can also recall the sinking feeling I had much later when my daughter revealed the truth of just why my dogs were trying to warn me.

Sleep has always been pretty darn enjoyable to me, but especially during those years, I needed to be at my mental and physical best. I worked long hours at my job as a supervisor in a Police/Fire/EMS dispatch center.

Life as a 911 public safety dispatcher was rewarding, but also very stressful and demanding, requiring quick thinking and mental agility.

We never knew what was at the end of the phone call...within minutes we could get calls ranging from a barking dog call, a house on fire, a multiple-vehicle collision with injuries, to someone who woke up to the sound of a window breaking, to a woman screaming in terror because her husband is beating the crap out of her. Each call had to be quickly prioritized and appropriate units sent.

In addition, the nature of the job demanded filling positions 24 hours a day, 7 days a week, resulting in a substantial amount of required overtime. Holidays and birthdays were just another day at the office for me.

As a single mom, I wanted to be "superwoman", to be omnipresent in my daughter's life. I also wanted to provide her with a home and the basic necessities, so choices had to be made. Many times, after working a busy shift, it could be challenging to switch from "work mode" to "mom mode" without some residual stress of the day spilling over. Even though my daughter was always pretty self-sufficient, balancing work life and home life sometimes felt like trying to juggle bowling balls.

My daughter and I have had our ups and downs, but we were always pretty close. However, when I came home from work for a quick lunch, and found a letter my 13-year-old daughter left for me that said...

"Mom, I'm pregnant, please don't be mad"

I was immediately thrown into a pit of shock and despair and felt like a total failure as a mom. How I managed to drive back to work and finish the day, I have no idea, it's still just a blur.

The thought of my daughter having to navigate the challenges of pregnancy and motherhood at such a young age was overwhelming.

So many thoughts, questions, and fears flew through my mind. She was so young, could she handle the physical demands of carrying a baby? My daughter was born two months premature, and due to the severity of my complications the doctors told my family I would not survive but they believed she would be okay. What if she went through what I did and didn't make it? Those thoughts were all I could think about until her doctor assured me that she would be okay. Apparently, he was convincing because I finally felt that I could breathe again.

The worry of her pregnancy was just the beginning – there was also school, caring for a baby, lost friendships, and the statistics facing teen mothers. On top of my worry for my daughter, I couldn't grasp how I was going to pay for the pregnancy and the added costs of the baby.

At 13, how was she going to navigate life and be required to make some serious grown-up decisions that will affect the rest of her life? It was hard for me to register, let alone accept it as reality.

It was a time full of the unknowns, fear of the future, and lots of emotions to process.

Needless to say, the rest of the year was like a roller coaster ride, but we got through it, and looking back there were so many pivotal moments, hard lessons learned, and a few legit miracles.

Had I gotten out of bed and investigated when my dogs were barking in the middle of the night, I might have stopped my daughter from her clandestine meetings. Since she was not old enough to date, sneaking out her window seemed a great option.

She told me later how she had to be extra careful, because many nights a member of my police family, would drive by our house and flash the lights over the windows. She would have to wait until they left, then jump out and hide in the bushes to make sure they had gone, and then keep a close watch in case they drove back by again.

We can "if only" all day long, but in the end, the reality is, we can't turn back the clock. Most of the time, with hindsight as our friend, we discover we wouldn't want to because everything happened as it should.

I found out fast, that grandkids are the best thing since sliced bread. I laugh now at how unnecessary all the agony, stress, and mental anguish was.

Living in the moments of that year, I dreaded the future and was overcome with fear of all the things that could go wrong, my daughter's life being ruined was on the list.

I wasn't focused on seeing anything good that year, I was wallowing in worry, self-pity, and shattered dreams.

What I thought would ruin her life, actually saved it. Later she told me that if it hadn't been for her daughter, she would have probably gone down a destructive path. However, with a new baby to care for, she was forced to grow up fast. Even at a young age, she recognized that she had to focus on changing her priorities and her future to provide a better life for her daughter. Her baby gave her a sense of purpose and direction. She went on to finish high school and college and earned a master's degree in counseling.

Today she is a successful, happy, and wonderful mother. During her college years, she met and married the love of her life, and they married and had my grandson.

Two grandkids are even better!!

My granddaughter now is married and has three littles of her own, making me a very young Great Grandmother.

I prayed a lot that year, prayers explaining just how I thought things should go. But in the end, the moment that little baby girl showed her face to the world I was madly in love. In those first few minutes, all the stress and agony of the past year not only slipped away, but it all seemed pointless. After all, no one can stop the wheels of life from turning, and trying to control what can't be controlled just brings heartache.

Planning for the future, and having dreams and goals to work towards is an excellent strategy for success. But in this case, I was so attached to the outcome and all the "what ifs", I lived in a constant state of doubt that either of us would get through it. Now my mission is to live life to its fullest, to look for joy in every moment, and trust the path I'm on. When obstacles come, I know with faith and trust in God, I will get through them.

There are a lot of definitions of work-life balance, but my experience has been that balance comes from within. The confidence that comes with knowing who you are and what you stand for will prepare you for those tough times.

I found that my priorities have changed over the years. Time with my family and doing the things I love to do is precious to me. I retired from public safety after 20 years and opened my own dog grooming business. Finally, I could dictate my own schedule and the first thing I declared was I would never work another holiday and only work on weekends if I felt like it.

In addition, I am a partner in an online marketing training and coaching business. Our mission is to train and equip people to navigate the online space to be able to grow and achieve success so they can have the time and financial freedom to live the life of their dreams.

I used to be proud of how "busy" I was. Until I realized being "busy" didn't really accomplish much. I found I could get more done in small amounts of focused time and have more time to play. To have lunch with a friend, ride my horse, play with my great-grandbabies, read a book, or just sit on my back porch and enjoy the morning.

We all have the same 24 hours, it's what we chose to do with those hours that make the difference. I have learned to say 'no' to a lot of things that I never thought I would. I also find I am selective with what I say "yes" to.

There are always things in our daily lives that can turn upside down, bills that need to be paid, family problems, and work struggles that occur. Having a side business or a full-time business can bring its own set of crazy into the mix.

Looking back, I can see that the events of that year gave me the chance to be a better mother, and eventually a better wife, grandmother, and great-grandmother. To understand what really matters in life, and to appreciate the power of love, family, and genuine friendships.

I currently live in the country with my husband, we have a collection of various farm animals that we adore. I love to travel with my horse, spending a weekend camping and riding the trails. By day we ride and at night we sit by the campfire and swap stories about horses and kids.

Between working two businesses, volunteer work, family, friends, fun, and daily chores. It's easy to fall back into the "I'm so busy" mindset.

To me it's not about trying to find time for work and family, it's about enjoying each moment you are in, slowing down, and letting the 'busy stuff' go. I'll admit to being a work in progress, there are times I've caught myself saying, "I'm too busy right now." I've learned to reframe those words to something like, "I am working on this right now, but in 30 minutes I am all yours."

Like many entrepreneurs, I am a big proponent of personal growth. I firmly believe that whatever life throws our way, we have been enabled and equipped by a loving God to face it head-on, and if we stumble it's part of the process and we get the choice to fail forward. Look at each day as a gift and make it your own personal masterpiece. Since we can't get back the past hours and days, why not focus on the right now and let go of all the regrets of yesterday and the worries of tomorrow?

Looking back, I can see that the events of that year gave me the chance to become a better mother, grandmother, and even great-grandmother and mentor. To understand what really matters in life, and to appreciate the power of love, family, and taking time out for fun.

The mission of Sherril & Tonia Coaching is to help home business owners take the overwhelm out of online marketing. So, they can create a solid content-to-sales conversion system that will allow them the freedom to live the life of their dreams doing what they love in work or play.

Check out these resources: https://member.toniasmith.com/links

My biz partner Sherril and I would love for you to join our Facebook group, *Social Media Marketing Made Simple & Fun*. Scan the code below for details as well as a roadmap that shows you the daily action steps to get leads, engagement and sales.

https://member.toniasmith.com/7-daily-actions-of-a-top-earner

Also, check out these resources: https://member.toniasmith.com/links

Lisa Wages

This chapter is dedicated to my kids Evan and Allison. Without them I wouldn't be the woman I am today. Love you always.

IT'S A MIRACLE THAT YOU ARE HERE. GOD MUST HAVE BIG PLANS FOR YOU.

Lisa Wages

And if I had a dollar for every time I've heard that… well let's just say we could take a fabulous trip to a fancy resort somewhere.

That's a big concept for a kid to feel they need to live up to though.

In 1971, I was born at 26 weeks gestation. That's not a big deal now, but way back then it was. The amazing part was there weren't any big complications then, just tiny at 2.5 lbs.

We did find out months later that I developed a vision impairment due to too much oxygen in an incubator. Totally not a big deal though.

From a young age, I decided that I was going to overcompensate for any perceived disability and prove to everyone that I was just like everyone else.

I became an overachiever as a kid which followed me for years. Being on the honor roll was my standard.

I became an early childhood special education teacher, and loved it. Being a caretaker came natural to me. I was all in as a teacher and advocate for my students which foreshadowed our journey.

Years later, my son was born, and I felt called to stay home with him. Maybe intuitively I knew trouble was ahead, but all was good until everything started to shift.

Evan got very sick at the age of 3 just as my daughter was born. He had his first grand mal seizure which landed him in the hospital on a ventilator. After that he lost the language he had and regressed socially. They labeled it autism, but truth be told I didn't care what it was called. I just wanted solutions.

I dove head first into being a special needs parent letting it consume me for over 16 years. Balance didn't exist because the kids came first no matter what.

The priority was healing the kids from their health struggles, so I took my first step toward boldness by walking away from a 12-year toxic marriage to an abusive narcissist. Sometimes I am still working to rebuild my confidence, from that situation, but taking that first step was huge.

I found the world of entrepreneurship feeling it was the answer to having a flexible career that allowed me to work around the kids. It did at first in many ways.

I knew that I didn't want to go back in a classroom, so learning to be successful as an online entrepreneur was critical. Trying to do it all "just right" cost me hours and hours of study, stress and a whole lot of money.

I don't know if it was the overwhelm of trying to do all things perfect or the hormonal shifts of Menopause, but I hit a brick wall. Exhaustion, an unexplained weight gain, and adrenal fatigue forced me to find answers.

As women and especially moms we often put our kids, our parents and even our work first before taking care of ourselves. That only works for so long before we end up sick, burnt out and honestly completely lost.

I've asked myself, who am I now anyway if I'm not taking care of somebody?

I began to wonder how do I balance the needs of my family, build my business, and keep my sanity.

Balancing work, family, and self-care can be a challenge. But it is possible to find balance in these areas while still finding success. With a little bit of effort and planning, you can create a life that is both meaningful and rewarding.

Achieving a healthy balance between work and life can be difficult when you're busy juggling multiple tasks. But it's important to remember that work should not consume all of your time or energy. Setting boundaries between work and home will help you stay focused during the day so that you can be more productive, while also ensuring that you have time to relax and spend with your family in the evenings.

Spending quality time with your family is essential for developing strong relationships with them. This includes taking time out of your day to talk to them about their lives, participating in activities together like going on walks or playing board games, sharing meals together, or simply just being there for them emotionally when they need it. Making an effort to connect with each member of your family individually will help foster strong bonds between everyone in the household.

The key to achieving success is taking care of yourself first before anything else. This means getting enough restful sleep at night so that you are energized during the day; eating healthily; exercising regularly; connecting with friends; engaging in hobbies; meditation or mindfulness practices; and having positive outlook on life. Regularly incorporating self-care into your daily routine will help keep you motivated and energized throughout the day while reducing stress levels at home and at work.

Finding balance in life does not necessarily mean achieving perfection but rather creating an environment where all aspects of life are working harmoniously together for overall success and fulfillment. By setting boundaries between work, family, and self-care, implementing routines that incorporate all three areas into everyday life, and making sure to prioritize yourself first before anything else, you will be able to create a balanced lifestyle that works best for you while still reaching your goals both personally and professionally.

As a mom and special needs caregiver, it can be easy to become overwhelmed. Finding balance between family, work and running a successful business is no small feat - the stress of managing all of these responsibilities can often lead to burnout

But with the right approach, life does not have to be an endless cycle of stress and exhaustion. By designing your life, you can create a lifestyle that works for you and your family, while still achieving success.

Take the time to prioritize the things that matter most to you - this could include quality time with family or taking care of yourself by getting enough rest. Make sure to build in breaks and space to take care of yourself, too. Utilize the resources available to help you create a plan that works - whether it's hiring an assistant or delegating work, don't be afraid to ask for help.

That's why now as a certified mental wellness and business coach, I help women feel healthier, happier and more confident so they can make more money. We get to the root cause problems they're facing and find simple holistic solutions to optimize the gut brain axis and implement the mindset tools so they can manifest the life of their dreams.

Connect with me here:

https://linktr.ee/Coachlisawages

BUSINESS SPOTLIGHT

Lil Barcaski, CEO
GWN Publishing, LLC
Virtual Creatives Marketing

OUR MISSION:

Writing for the Greater Good

For the last 15 years, Lil has been the CEO and project manager of a publishing and marketing firm based out of the Tampa Bay area and a much sought-after ghostwriter and consultant. She has ghostwritten dozens of books in the business, memoir, and even fiction genres. Lil is an author, playwright, blogger, coach, and consultant.

As CEO of GWN Publishing/Virtual Creatives, she heads up a staff of writers, editors, designers, and publishing experts.

GWN Publishing offers ghostwriting, editing, and publishing services. We can create websites and marketing materials for authors, speakers, and small businesses. We also specialize in the best and most cost-effective way to produce compilation books.

We work with entrepreneurs, coaches, and consultants who want to elevate their business profile by writing and speaking on their business topic and zone of genius.

Our newest program is "From Pen to Published" and includes, one-on-one coaching, proofreading and a full publishing package.

Life by Design discount - $500 discount ($3,997 reg price) – $3,497.

EMAIL: lil@Ghostwritersnetwork.com to learn more.

BUSINESS SPOTLIGHT

Kim Ward
Life By Design Solutions

Kim Ward is a digital marketing strategist who helps driven entrepreneurs kick ass and find their fire. When you work with Kim, you will no longer feel defeated. You can make decisions that move you closer to your goals instead of sleepwalking through your day.

With the right mindset, you will create your life and business by design. But it's not just about mindset—Kim's expertise in marketing will help you leverage your time and resources and end the days of feeling overwhelmed and overworked.

With Kim's approach, you'll learn how to have fun while growing your business. Use the QR code and connect with her.

CPSIA information can be obtained
at www.ICGtesting.com
Printed in the USA
JSHW071250020623
42629JS00007B/132

9 781959 608325